#1 INTERNATIONAL BEST SELLER

ALPHAS DIE EARLY

FOR THE MAN ON A MISSION AND THE WOMEN WHO LOVE HIM

DAVE ROSSI
Commentary by Brad Kearns

ALPHAS DIE EARLY

FOR THE MAN ON A MISSION
AND THE WOMEN WHO LOVE HIM

DAVE ROSSI

Dave Rossi © Copyright 2026
Book Layout ©2026 www.EvolveGlobalPublishing.com

No part of this book may be reproduced or transmitted in any form or by any means, electronic or mechanical, including photocopying, recording or by any information storage and retrieval system, without written permission from the authors, except for the inclusion of brief quotations in a review..

Limit of Liability Disclaimer: The information contained in this book is for information purposes only and may not apply to your situation. The author, publisher, distributor, and provider provide no warranty about the content or accuracy of the content enclosed. The information provided is subjective. Keep this in mind when reviewing this guide. Neither the Publisher nor the Author shall be liable for any profit loss or other commercial damages resulting from using this guide. All links are for information purposes only and are not warranted for content, accuracy, or any other implied or explicit purpose.

This book is not intended as a substitute for medical advice. The reader should regularly consult a physician in matters relating to their health, particularly concerning any symptoms that may require diagnosis or medical attention.

No part of this book may be used or reproduced in any manner for the purpose of training artificial intelligence technologies or systems. In accordance with Article 4(3) of the Digital Single Market Directive 2019/790, Evolve Global Publishing expressly reserves this work from the text and data mining exception..

TRADEMARKS

All product names, logos, and brands are the property of their respective owners. All company, product, and service names used in this book are for identification purposes only. Using these names, logos, and brands does not imply endorsement. All other trademarks cited herein are the property of their respective owners..

Alphas Die Early: *For the Man on a Mission — And the Women Who Love Him*
1st Edition. 2026 ver. 2

ASIN: B0GF6XYRQG (Amazon Kindle)
ISBN: 978-1-923223-77-6 (Amazon) PAPERBACK
ISBN: 978-1-923223-79-0 (Amazon) HARDCOVER
ISBN: 978-1-923223-78-3 (Ingram Spark) PAPERBACK
ISBN: 978-1-923223-80-6 (Ingram Spark) HARDCOVER
ISBN: 978-1-923223-75-2 (Ebook))

CONTACT THE AUTHOR:

Facebook: https://www.facebook.com/daverossiglobal/
Instagram: https://www.instagram.com/daverossiglobal/
Youtube: https://www.youtube.com/channel/UCWSsEcaN1g8FmnoNbMMLlww
Website: https://getmybook.store/s/alphas
Email: rossi.dbr@gmail.com

Font & Styles:
Style - L
Header: Archer 25pt
Font Size: Content - Avenir 11pt

Table of Contents

Letter to the Reader	7
Introduction	11
Part I: Understanding the Problem	**19**
Chapter 1: The Problem with the "Real Man"	21
Chapter 2: Why We Need a New Definition of Masculinity	41
Chapter 3: Fear —The Hidden Driver of Masculinity	51
Vector of Self-Mastery	63
Part II: Breaking the Cycle	**69**
Chapter 4: A New Masculinity — The Non-Masculine Male	71
Chapter 5: Recognizing the Scripts to Break — Relationships & Childhood Programming	85
Chapter 5: Redefining Success	101
Part III: The Transition	**121**
Chapter 7: Letting Go of the Mask	123
Chapter 8: Why It's Worth it	149
Chapter 9: Learn to Live with Purpose and Freedom	165

Part IV: Secret Playbook of The Omega — **181**

    Chapter 10: The Basics – A Roadmap for Sustained Growth — 183

    Chapter 11: The Playbook – Spiritual Behaviors to Live By — 203

    Chapter 12: The Challenges & The Spiritual Strength of the Omega Code — 231

Conclusion: The Return of the Man Who Became Himself — **251**

Letter to the Reader

From the author: A letter to every man who's ever felt like he was failing at being a man

There was a day, years ago, when I stood at the edge of a second-story window and truly wondered if jumping would be less painful than staying. I was not suicidal. But remembering that moment I considered it — as I'm sure many have — hit me hard.

The excruciating weight of that moment didn't come out of nowhere. It came after years of trying to do the "right thing" for my marriage, business, family, and identity. I had achieved everything I thought I was supposed to: I built the dream home, made millions, married the Ivy League intellect, started a company, had the kids, and bought the boat, the building, and the flashy things. But inside, I was dying; I was maybe even already dead inside.

I didn't know it then, but I was living a programmed life. One built from early wiring, from being told I was "too sensitive," feeling invisible in my own home, and learning that love had to be earned through loyalty, sacrifice, and performance. I was an Enneagram 2 through and through — always helping, always fixing. I tested as an INFJ personality type (introverted, intuitive, feeling, and judging), and sometimes ENFJ (extroverted, intuitive, feeling, and judging).

For context, the ENFJ is one of sixteen personality types identified by the Myers-Briggs Type Indicator (MBTI), a widely used tool that helps individuals better understand how they perceive the world and make decisions. Sometimes called "The Protagonist," an ENFJ is typically found to be empathetic, driven by purpose, and wired to help others. It's not a label, but a lens that helped me better understand the patterns I was trying to outgrow and the ones worth keeping. Both ENFJ and INFJ are deeply feeling and other-focused types.

Over time, those strengths became chains. I stayed in broken relationships far too long. I tolerated betrayal, emotional volatility, and even financial ruin to avoid being the one who hurt someone else. I lost myself in the process. And yet, through inner work, I gained something much more profound.

That day at the window didn't end with a jump. It ended with a vow to find a better way. That path became my first book, The Imperative Habit, where I rebuilt myself one behavior at a time. I found practices that grounded me, pulled me out of despair, and gave me clarity. But even then, something deeper still needed to shift. Something else needed to come out.

That's what *Alphas Die Early* is about.

This book is not just a follow-up — it's a shedding. A shedding of every role I thought I had to play. The Alpha who dominates. The Fixer who saves. The Son who pleases. The Man who suffers in silence. These were not just roles I played; they were survival strategies. But survival isn't the same as being alive.

It took me years — long, messy, painful years — to understand how deeply those patterns were embedded. I worked with therapists, spiritual teachers, and even energy workers like Judith Swack, who helped me uncover the invisible emotional contracts I didn't even know I'd signed.

Slowly, I started to unearth the truth: that who I am is not who I was told to be. I could choose a life guided by spiritual principles, not just social programming. And that masculinity, or what it meant to be a "Real Man," could be defined by presence and purpose, not power.

That's why I wrote this book — not just to share what I've learned but to give others the roadmap I never had. If you're reading this and some part of you feels trapped by a role, a relationship, or a version of yourself you can't escape, I want you to know there's a way out.

You are not broken. You are buried. You, too, may be living programs you are not aware of, and they run deeper than you can imagine.

This is the unearthing. The breaking free. The climb out of the burrow. If my story means anything, let it be this: You don't have to be the Alpha. You don't have to win, dominate, or prove anything. You have to discover who you already are underneath it all. In the same way that gravity was already there before Sir Isaac Newton discovered it, who you are underneath it all is already there, waiting for you to discover it.

That's where your power lives. That's where real freedom begins.

With love,

Dave Rossi

Introduction

The call: a 'hero's journey - recognizing the crisis of masculinity

You wake up at the age of 40 and realize you're not living the life you'd intended for yourself. Or you're 24 years old and fear you're going in the wrong direction. Or maybe you're 60 and feel empty, wishing you had more to reflect your legacy.

You followed all the rules. You achieved success, respect, and admiration. And yet, inside, you feel something is missing; maybe you even feel hollow, like you're living a life you didn't choose. One that fell short of being a man. Remiss in your own understanding of masculinity and success.

If you feel this way, you're not alone. Men are silently falling apart. We hide behind so many things: ambition, competition, bravado, and even repression or silence because no one taught us any different. The real tragedy isn't just that we're struggling. It's that we're still trying to figure out how to be a man in today's world with yesterday's tools and ideals related to masculinity.

This book is not about fixing you. You are not broken. It's about freeing you from a program, a survival script wired into your biology and culture that was never designed for fulfillment, only for a perpetual need for domination, competition, and survival. It's time to evolve.

Don't believe me? Look around. Men are in trouble.

Young men lead alarming trends in mental health decline. In 2022, 36.2% of young adults aged 18–25 were diagnosed with a mental health condition, the highest rate of any age group. Even more concerning, 11.6% reported serious mental illnesses. Studies also show that young men face higher rates of loneliness and fewer social connections, contributing to increased suicide rates. And it doesn't stop there.

Economically, men are falling behind. Women's earnings and educational achievements have grown steadily over the last decade, while men's progress has stagnated. This is not a bad thing, and it represents the continued evolution of society beyond the dated gender stereotypes of past generations. Irrespective of women rising, men are still stagnating. In 2021, men received only 42% of bachelor's degrees, the lowest on record. These statistics aren't just numbers; they represent real men, real lives unraveling under the weight of unmet expectations and silent struggles.

I'm not just yapping from the peanut gallery. I've risen and fallen dramatically over the past few decades. By the time I was in my mid-forties, I had everything a 'real man' or Alpha is supposed to have: money, success, and a family. But I was miserable. I didn't feel like a man, let alone the Alpha male I seemed to be portraying in Silicon Valley society. I had followed the script of masculinity society handed me, and still, something was missing.

What happened to us?

It's easy to point fingers. We blame the system, the rise of females in competitive education, maybe the economy, woke ideology, DEI policies, our parents' imperfections, or even the roles our friends or significant others play in our lives.

But what if the problem isn't "out" there? What if it's "inside" us? Could *we* be the problem?

For years, I rationalized my failures. I blamed others. I convinced myself that my lack of success was someone else's fault; that the system was rigged, or people were jealous of me. It was too painful to admit that maybe I wasn't living the way I needed to. I was following a script written for me by others, not by myself.

It took me hitting ROCK bottom before I realized everything I was taught or knew, to that point, was wrong. I learned there were other ways, not the "same ole' way" everyone told me I had to follow.

Certainly not the way society deemed as "the way." In the beginning, it taught me that blame was not the answer. I know the cost of staying trapped. It cost me my peace, my relationships, my sense of self, and my future. But it also became my catalyst.

Every incredible journey begins with a moment of reckoning, when the life we built becomes too small for the life we're called to live.

So, what changed for me?

How did I switch onto a path of peace, ease, and enlightenment? (It's not dogmatic enlightenment; it's just a word denoting heavy introspection and self-realization). As Joseph Campbell, the author of *The Hero with a Thousand Faces*, puts it, it's the archetypal path of transformation: an individual is called to adventure, faces trials and crises, undergoes deep personal change, and returns with newfound wisdom to share with the world.

Did you know Joseph Campbell helped write the *Star Wars* script? George Lucas asked him to assist. Star Wars is a story of transformation. Many characters had their own "Hero's Journey" in the original trilogy.

Campbell says that, for centuries, stories have guided men on their path to transformation. From mythological heroes to modern-day legends, every great man has followed the same cycle: one of struggle, crisis, and self-discovery. Men don't need a new identity. They need to come home to the one they abandoned.

> *"The privilege of a lifetime is to become who you truly are."*
> **– Carl Jung**

This is what Campbell called the Hero's Journey, and whether we realize it or not, we are all living it. But what happens when the world no longer asks men to be heroes? What happens when, instead of crossing into the unknown, we stay trapped in a story that no longer serves us?

That's where I was stuck in a rut and feeling a deep sense of emptiness. What I needed was a path, a purpose; something beyond survival. I needed to enter the next phase of the journey.

My abyss: the catalyst for change

David Politi was the kind of man everyone admired: strong, charismatic, and seemingly untouchable. He'd been my BFF since 1977 and died suddenly in an accident in 2012. I was devastated. I carried the weight of his passing for five years, allowing myself to spiral downward, both practically and spiritually.

Soon after David's passing, I lost my business, marriage, and home. Even my physical health began to deteriorate. Everything that had defined me as a successful man was gone. And in that abyss, I had to face the terrifying reality: I'd spent my life chasing a version of masculinity that was never truly mine. If I was going to rebuild, it was going to have to be from the ground up.

David's death drowned me in sorrow until I finally realized that it wasn't just a tragic event burdening my life every waking moment, but a catalyst for my awakening. I'd not only lost a friend but a part of myself. It forced me to ask: If someone as solid as David could be taken so suddenly, what did that mean for the rest of us? Looking back now, his passing was not just a testament to him but to my own power that was drawn from pain, sorrow, and a willingness to grow. It was my initiation into something greater. My next step. My call to adventure, as Campbell would put it.

The Omega Man

It's easy to say we don't want someone's death to mean anything, but it takes immense courage to do something about it. It takes courage to live in a way that honors them, and to allow their life and their memory to shape our lives in a meaningful way. Most people stay stuck in their pain, never allowing themselves to find meaning beyond it. We all have pain. Maybe this pain has caused young men to drop off so precipitously in life.

For thousands of years, storytellers have returned to the figure of Odysseus, not because he was the strongest hero, but because he was the most evolved. He survives where others fall because he leads with awareness instead of aggression, humility instead of ego, and strategy instead of bravado. Joseph Campbell saw *The Odyssey* by Homer as one of the clearest expressions of the Hero's Journey, but Odysseus also reveals something deeper: he is an ancient embodiment of the Omega path. His trials force him to shed pride, confront himself, and return home transformed not more dominant, but more conscious. The Omega Man is cut from that same lineage. He is the man who stops performing and starts becoming.

With Christopher Nolan's upcoming film The Odyssey – starring Matt Damon as Odysseus and set for release on July 17, 2026, this connection between myth, transformation, and modern masculinity becomes even more compelling.

After losing everything, I eventually discovered my power. And I now have the opportunity to honor David's life and pass on the wisdom I've gained because of him. For that, I want to introduce The Omega Man Manifesto:

> *"The greatest test of the Omega Man is this: to emerge from the abyss and take what one has learned and live it. To show and motivate others so they can find their own new way, not by force, not by judgment or superiority, but by example, with support and strength."*

Like Campbell's hero, Nietzsche's Übermensch in his book Zarathustra, or Krishna in the Bhagavad Gita, the Omega Man is called to rise not with force but with wisdom. These stories aren't just old; they're blueprints for a new way to live.

Nietzsche's Übermensch is the ideal human who rises above the herd, beyond outdated morality, cultural programming, and the need for external approval. He doesn't follow the rules. He creates them. He lives with radical independence, forging meaning from within. However, what Nietzsche called "strength" lacked something essential: heart. Compassion. Self-mastery, not just of power, but of fear, emotion, and ego. The Omega Man is not a rejection of Nietzsche's vision but its evolution. He is, in essence, the modern embodiment of the Übermensch, updated for a world that no longer needs domination but demands transformation.

Why this book?

I did not invent The Omega Man. I remembered him. He's what Campbell saw, what Zarathustra declared in Nietzsche's Thus Spoke Zarathustra, and what Krishna called Arjuna to become in the Bhagavad Gita: the man who sees clearly, acts purposefully, and lives from spirit.

And as such, this book isn't here to shame you. It's here to free you. For decades, we have been sold a lie about what it means to be a man; one that suffocates our potential and disconnects us from our true selves. This isn't about rejecting masculinity. It's about redefining it. Masculinity is built on self-mastery, purpose, and authenticity. Masculinity is yours; it's not someone else's script. This is not just a book, it's a mirror and a map.

If you've ever felt the silent ache of living someone else's definition of strength, you're already on the path. This book will help you complete the journey.

The return from the abyss

Every hero must face the abyss, but not every man finds his way back. Some get stuck in failure, some in regret, some in grief, and some in the labels or archetypes, like the Alpha, that they won't let go of.

The key to my return was understanding that absolute masculinity isn't about pretending to be strong. It's about becoming strong by embracing who you really are, not someone or something you're pretending to be. Like Campbell's Hero's Journey, each person must discover their own form of self and their own form of masculinity. This book will unfold like a path of markers, showing you how to discover what you need to understand and what it means to be authentically you.

The new man: the Omega Man

Enter the Omega Man: an evolved, freer, more empowering version of the traditional archetypes of masculinity. Unlike the Alpha, who seeks dominance and leadership, the Beta, who conforms and follows, or even the Sigma, who seeks independence, the Omega seeks self-mastery.

What to expect

Through personal stories, spiritual insights, and practical tools, you'll be provided with a playbook to shed the harmful aspects of traditional masculinity and embrace a deeper, more fulfilling way of living.

This isn't just about changing yourself. It's about transforming your entire way of being.

> **Reflections from Brad Kearns — Reader, Friend, Biohacker, Author, and Fellow Traveler on This Path**

Since I recently turned 60, I definitely connected with this section from the very first paragraph! Recall it ended with, "Or maybe you're 60 and feel empty, wishing you had more to reflect your legacy."

I celebrated my 60th birthday with a great gathering of family and friends, so I certainly didn't feel "empty" on that occasion. However, when you get to be 60 and have been driving hard in the competitive arena for decades, some difficult reflections often happen.

I'm at the age where I can look around and notice a good percentage of my friends and peers retiring, or otherwise slowing down and enjoying the fruits of their hard labor and long climb up the corporate ladder/asset accumulation ladder. For competitive types, it's easy to start stressing about the big scoreboard at age 60 - the scoreboard of life - then decide to feel inferior or agitated about why things haven't gone according to big dreams.

I appreciate Dave being able to bare his soul and talk openly about hitting rock bottom and deciding what to do about it. This makes it easier for all of us to talk openly about difficult subjects, do some honest reflection without feeling like a dork, and hopefully evolve and grow from reflections instead of just feeling lousy.

Part I:

Understanding the Problem

Chapter 1:

The Problem with the "Real Man"

Before we dive deep into the roots of this crisis, I want you to pause for a moment and ask yourself something: If you're a "real man" or an Alpha, how do you think it should feel inside?

- Should it feel like strength or survival?

- Should it feel like freedom, or fear of something?

- Should it be a mask you wear, or a truth you live?

Before we define masculinity with studies and stories, we need to admit to the feelings most men carry.

Despite all the performance, all the striving, all the pretending, something about the traditional definition never quite fits; it appears to be a standard I cannot quite reach. Always striving, never arriving.

Right? Do you feel like you are constantly trying to "prove" your life's achievements lest society challenge your masculinity?

If someone asked you to define what makes a "real man," or Alpha, would you know how to answer?

Okay, what is it?

Tell yourself now and see how well that holds up. In fact, please write it down and look at it after you finish this book. See what you were thinking when you wrote it down, and then check again after you've finished reading.

For generations, men have been shaped to repress their emotions, dominate their environment, and define their worth by their achievements, wealth, and power. The history of "fleecing" manhood is explained in greater detail in Chapter 4. Until then, it has been no secret that the cultural narrative of what it means to be an Alpha has infiltrated every aspect of our lives, from the playground to the boardroom.

To make this point clearer, reflect on the following:

- Have you ever acted tough and competitive, and suppressed emotion because you thought that was what was expected of you?

- Have you ever felt compelled or socially pressured to act in a way propagated by others that followed ideas of what was thought to be a real man?

Of course, we've all felt pressure and confusion, and we've even acted on what we felt it meant to be a real man. I'm here to tell you that this confusion cuts deeper than we think.

It's not just that the expectations are unrealistic; it's that they are built on a definition supported by shifting sand.

One generation defines manhood by domination, another by wealth, and another by stoic silence. Each time the definition changes, the millions of men tracking it are left scrambling, exhausted, and lost as to what the new definition is and whether that definition is the final word. How often do you think the nuances of the definition have changed? A lot.

We should not be surprised that men are tired. It's no wonder so many are quietly collapsing under the invisible weight they carry to be a real man or Alpha male.

Understanding the Problem

I see two major pitfalls with the confusion surrounding this masculine archetype or stereotype:

- The definition of a "Real Man" is not universal. (It's not even the same between social settings.)

- Albeit not universally defined, men are REQUIRED to meet the standard of masculinity, or risk not being an Alpha.

No wonder so many men feel trapped, disconnected, and, at times, deeply unhappy. They cannot meet the definition of being a real man when one does not exist. However, the pressure to be a "Real Man" is all around them!

To be an Alpha: at best, a moving target

The recent "real man" or Alpha Male archetype is rooted in societal expectations. Currently, and in the U.S. generally, boys are taught from an early age that crying is a sign of weakness, that vulnerability makes them "less than," and that their value lies in their ability to succeed and provide. This rigid framework leaves no room for individuality, emotional connection, or self-discovery.

What is more, different ethnicities and socio-economic classes have created subclasses of masculine gender role types. This makes the framework even more challenging to follow. Take a trip across the United States, and you will find that what it means to be a "real man" can vary as much as the landscape. In New York City, being a man might involve mastering the subway system and knowing the difference between a flat white and a cortado. Meanwhile, in Texas, being a real man could mean wrangling cattle under the scorching sun and knowing your way around a barbecue pit.

However, this is not just geography within a single country. When you travel to different parts of the world, you'll see masculinity takes on different shades. In Japan, the concept of masculinity is often defined with woven aspects of stoicism and a staunch dedication to work. In Brazil, on the other hand, it might be celebrated through the exuberance of carnival dancers and soccer players.

If masculinity can look so different across cultures, why does it feel like we're all supposed to fit into a single mold? Why do we still hear the same phrases — 'man up,' 'do not cry,' 'be a provider' — no matter where we are? This contradiction is not just frustrating, it's isolating. When men don't fit the script, they don't just feel different; they feel like failures.

Emotional checkpoint: Before you keep reading, pause and check in. Ask yourself, "Where have I worn a mask of masculinity recently? Was it today?"

The opposite sex and the masculine broken mirror

Let's talk about the opposite sex's view on masculine roles. They are the yin to our yang, the sugar to our spice, and sometimes, the wrench in our quest to be a "real man". Their expectations, desires, and even their disinterest can send us spinning faster than a top in a Beyblade tournament. One minute, we're trying to impress them with our rugged charm; the next, we wonder if they find sensitivity more attractive than six-pack abs. Similarly, it changes from potential suitor to suitor, often based on what masculine attributes they found successful (or not) in past relationships.

When they don't know, how can we?

The performance of the actor 'Alpha' – at a masquerade ball

Let's not forget the social media aspect — the digital hall of mirrors that reflects a thousand versions of masculinity, each more filtered and Photoshopped than the last. From Instagram influencers flaunting their #blessed lives to X, formerly known as Twitter, threads debating the merits of beard oil versus mustache wax, it's easy to get lost in the noise. The only clear and firm understanding of what the opposite sex says about masculinity is that there isn't one.

I remember one such experience, and maybe this has happened to you. I thought being emotionally distant made me more attractive because that's what I'd seen recently in movies, but I also felt it would work with this particular girl. But then, another woman overheard me. Based on what she eventually told her friend, she appeared to understand what I was trying to portray — emotionally unavailable, and aloof, as I'd planned. The woman who overheard me told her friend that she wished I were 'more open' and 'more vulnerable.' One woman valued strength. The other valued softness. I felt so stupid. I'd pretended to be someone I wasn't, only to find that, had I just been myself, it might have worked!

Maybe it was because Jon Rodriguez was around — the known "bad boy" who got all the girls with his brooding, tightly held emotions, and bravado.

What the hell was I supposed to do? Was I supposed to be the strong, silent type or the sensitive poet?

The truth is, most women don't know exactly what they want in a man either, and that's part of the problem. The definition keeps changing, even from girl to girl in the same circle!

Masculinity and biology: science and society collide

Studies in evolutionary psychology have found that a woman's preferences for masculine traits can fluctuate based on where they are in their menstrual cycle. For example, during the fertile phase of the cycle, women tend to prefer more masculine male features, such as strong jawlines, deep voices, and dominant behavior, likely due to subconscious associations with genetic fitness and short-term mating potential[1]. In contrast, during non-fertile phases, women are more drawn to traits associated with emotional warmth and long-term partnership. This shift becomes even more pronounced in environments with higher disease or risk of violence, where stronger masculine traits are perceived as more protective or advantageous[2].

The concept of masculinity is also closely tied to the cultural expectations of gender roles. Social role theory suggests that societal norms dictate appropriate behaviors for men and women, leading

---

References

1. DeBruine et al., 2010
2. Marcinkowska et al., 2021

individuals to align with these expectations in ways that can reinforce traditional gender roles[3]. Furthermore, the sociological theory of "doing gender" highlights how individuals actively perform behaviors aligned with societal gender norms, reinforcing existing gender structures[4]. This can result in men adopting behaviors they believe are attractive to women, even when these behaviors perpetuate outdated or harmful traits.

So, not only does the definition of attractiveness change from woman to woman, it can literally shift within the same woman depending on her biology and environment. How the hell are men supposed to calibrate to that? Maybe we're not meant to. Maybe the goal isn't to adapt to every expectation, but to stop performing altogether.

Masculinity for sale: making money on confusion

Advertising plays a substantial role in perpetuating these stereotypes. Companies spend billions each year carefully developing campaigns that reinforce traditional notions of masculinity, whether it's the rugged outdoorsman or the suave businessman. In 2021 alone, over $5 billion was spent globally on advertising that specifically targeted men, promoting everything from cars and cologne to gym memberships and grooming products[5].

This bombardment of idealized images can have detrimental effects on young men. Studies show a correlation between exposure to idealized media portrayals of masculinity and negative body image, increased aggression, and lower self-esteem[6].

For example, in January 2019, Gillette launched an ad campaign, "The Best A Man Can Be," addressing issues like bullying, sexism, and toxic

---

References

    3. Eagly & Wood, 2012

    4. West & Zimmerman, 1987

    5. Statista

    6. American Psychological Association

masculinity. While some praised the campaign for challenging harmful male behaviors, it also faced significant backlash from individuals who felt it unfairly criticized traditional masculinity. I was a young man when this ad came out. And yes — I wanted to be the best a man could be. But what did that mean? And what if I didn't become that? What did it mean for me? (If you read the introduction to this book, you know how it turned out for me. Not good.)

This reaction illustrates the contentious nature of discussions surrounding male identity and the cultural resistance to redefining masculinity. But it also highlights how subtle it all is — in advertising and everyday life.

Nevertheless, if you, as a man, agree, then buy this product.

What a hook! "The best a man can be" depends on how close his shave is?

Should that be what defines a man? Trim facial hair? A beard? This is a further example of the perpetuation of these stereotypes and the confusion for young men about what it is to be a man.

There is an immediate need to address these issues — the problem and the solution — not through fear or blame, but by rewriting the narrative to create healthier, more inclusive definitions of masculinity. To create a definition to help you, as a man, find real steps toward growth, success, and better relationships.

The rise of toxic masculinity in online influencer culture

Andrew Tate, a former kickboxer and social media influencer, has been widely criticized for promoting misogynistic views. His content, which includes statements that demean women and endorse traditional gender roles, has gained significant traction among young men. Some of his most controversial statements include:

- *"I think the women belong to the men."* (women's autonomy)

- Tate has suggested that if a woman accuses a man of cheating, the appropriate response is to *"bang out the machete, boom in her face, and grip her by the neck."* (violence against women)

- *"I am absolutely a misogynist."* (gender roles)

This rhetoric not only perpetuates harmful stereotypes but also reinforces toxic masculinity as a path to power and validation for some young men. Tate's appeal lies in his self-vocalized success, promoting a "winning" mentality where adherence to his worldview defines one's status as either an alpha winner or a beta loser[7].

Other influencers promoting similar narratives

The "Manosphere" Community

The manosphere is a loosely connected online subculture that includes men's rights activists (MRAs), pick-up artists (PUAs), and incels (involuntary celibates). These groups promote an idealized version of hyper-masculinity while frequently advocating for the subjugation of women. Research suggests that young men immersed in these communities often develop adversarial beliefs about gender relations, viewing feminism and women's empowerment as direct threats to male status[8].

Kevin Samuels and the "High-Value Man" Concept

Kevin Samuels, a self-proclaimed dating and lifestyle coach, gained popularity for advising men on becoming "high-value." His content often reinforced traditional gender hierarchies, arguing that women should prioritize submission and that men should seek power through dominance via financial and social avenues. Although his content was not as overtly violent as Tate's, his messaging reinforced rigid gender norms, with statements such as:

- *"Men do not care about your degrees. They care about your beauty and your youth."*

- *"Women over 35 with children are leftovers in the dating market."*

References

7. Ging, 2019
8. Marwick & Caplan, 2018

These views normalize an outdated framework where women are valued primarily for their attractiveness and youth, while men are judged solely on financial prowess (Cruz, 2021).

Jordan Peterson's Traditionalism and its Misinterpretation

Jordan Peterson, a clinical psychologist and author, also appears to influence young men seeking guidance on masculinity. While Peterson's work, such as 12 Rules for Life, advocates for personal responsibility and self-discipline, many of his followers have taken his critiques of feminism and social progress as justification for regressive gender roles. His discussions about hierarchy and biological determinism have been weaponized by extreme groups within the manosphere, reinforcing the idea that men must reclaim traditional dominance in society (Kelly, 2019).

The impact of these influences

The proliferation of figures like Tate, Samuels, and Peterson, though distinct in their approaches, has a measurable impact on social behavior and gender perceptions. Oddly, it is the hamster wheel of bravado and perception of strength and success that created their peak, and their peak or perceived success that then supported their bravado to suggest others to follow.

It creates:

- **Normalization of misogyny** – Repeated exposure to such content desensitizes individuals, making sexist attitudes appear normal or even aspirational (Ging, 2019). This normalization is the backbone of the downward statistics proving young men's decline in almost every category.

- **Radicalization of youth** – Studies indicate that young men, particularly those feeling isolated or struggling with identity, are highly susceptible to radicalization through online communities promoting toxic masculinity (Marwick & Caplan, 2018).

- **Undermining gender equality** – These ideologies slow societal progress by reinforcing rigid power dynamics between men and women (Connell & Messerschmidt, 2005). These power struggles perpetuate the inability of young men to maintain positive relationships with women, as you will see in statistical form later in this chapter.

A tragic consequence of confused masculinity

An example of where the current perception of masculinity has turned toxic is the mass shooting in Isla Vista, California. The May 2014 rampage by Elliot Rodger resulted in six deaths and fourteen injuries before Rodger took his own life. The note left behind, a manifesto, expressed deep-seated misogyny and frustration over his perceived rejection by women, highlighting the dangers of internalized toxic masculinity and the emotional toll it can take on young men. (Elliot Rodger's Manifesto, "My Twisted World: The Story of Elliot Rodger," available at DocumentCloud, and NPR's article "A Killer's Manifesto Reveals Wide Reach of Misogyny Online," available at NPR.)

Was Elliot's rampage a result of his failing to follow Andrew Tate and others' rhetoric?

Based on the additional examples below, the data suggests it was. I'm not sharing these examples to be shocking but to provide real-world examples where toxic masculinity, or the confusion of being an Alpha, is affecting young men. These are not isolated incidents.

The phenomenon of toxic masculinity has been implicated in several violent incidents beyond the Isla Vista shooting by Elliot Rodger. Notable examples include:

- **Toronto Van Attack (2018)**

    Alek Minassian drove a van into pedestrians in Toronto, killing ten and injuring sixteen. Before the attack, he posted on Facebook expressing allegiance to the "incel" community, praising Elliot Rodger and announcing the "Incel Rebellion." This act highlighted the potential for misogynistic ideologies to manifest in mass violence. (Hoffman, B., Ware, J., & Shapiro, E. (2020). *Assessing the Threat of Incel Violence*. Georgetown Institute for Women, Peace, and Security. Georgetown University.)

- **Toronto Machete Attack (2020)**

    A 17-year-old male attacked workers at a Toronto massage parlor with a machete, resulting in one death and serious injuries to another. Investigations revealed the perpetrator was inspired by incel ideology, marking the first instance in Canada where an act of violence motivated by misogynistic beliefs was prosecuted as terrorism. (Perry, B. & Scrivens, R. (2022). *Right-Wing Extremism in Canada*: Assessing the Impact of Incel Ideology. Canadian Journal of Criminology and Criminal Justice, 64(2), 115-138.)

- **Plymouth Shooting (2021)**

    Jake Davison killed five individuals, including his mother, in Plymouth, UK, before taking his own life. Davison had expressed affiliation with incel culture and frequently posted online about his struggles with women and feelings of rejection, underscoring the dangers of internalized toxic masculinity. (Davies, C. (2021). *Plymouth Shooter's Ties to Incel Culture and the Dangers of Online Radicalization*. The Guardian, August 2021.)

One of the most striking portrayals of this crisis is in the recent Netflix miniseries Adolescence, created by Stephen Graham. The show follows a 13-year-old boy, Jamie, who becomes entangled in online radicalization and ultimately commits a horrifying act of violence. It is not just a crime drama; it's a mirror reflecting the confusion and pain many young men feel when trying to define what being a "real man" means.

In an interview with CNN's Christiane Amanpour, Graham said, "The internet is parenting our children just as much as we are." While I respect his work and the series' impact, I do not entirely agree with that statement. The real problem is not that the internet is parenting our kids; it is that boys are trying to figure out what mask to wear, and the internet provides access to so many masks and figures to follow instantly.

The mask is not the solution – it's the problem

It's not the internet that creates confusion because the confusion already exists. It's the mixed messages boys get about who they are supposed to be: "Strong, but gentle," "Tough, but sensitive," "Assertive, but not aggressive". This chaos of competing archetypes is parenting our children and teaching them to wear masks that do not fit. The real solution is not limiting screen time – that would only be a form of coping with the problem. The solution is to teach them not to wear a mask at all! I define this as authenticity.

It's important to teach our children to recognize what a mask is, the harm it can cause them, and ultimately, how ineffective and unsustainable it is.

Authenticity is not something you download. It's something you live. As long as we allow these cultural masks of masculinity to define our worth by our behaviors, or lack thereof, we'll keep seeing the fallout: confused young men trying to survive in roles they were never meant to play.

Let's keep going.

Masculinity as a political seduction for power

On TikTok and in political discourse, everyone seems to have a view on what it means to be a "real man," especially in relation to voting in the 2024 Presidential election. What makes this discussion so interesting and confusing is how the political landscape shapes and is shaped by the definition of gender roles. Masculinity has nothing to do with political policies or positions, yet it often becomes deeply entwined with them.

Polls shifting from Trump/Vance to Harris/Walz revealed two key dynamics:

1. Masculine gender roles were attached to each party's ticket.
2. The Harris/Walz ticket represented a broader definition, a more inclusive view of masculinity.

Understanding the Problem

Meanwhile, Trump/Vance reflected a brash, unapologetic style and a narrower definition more closely tied to male dominance.

Having a political view can be seen as an extremely divisive attack on one's masculinity, depending on the audience. Donald Trump has frequently tied masculinity to dominance and power, as reflected in controversial statements. For example:

- In 2005, Trump said, "Grab'em by the pussy," boasting about his ability to sexually assault women due to his celebrity status. "When you are a star, they let you do it. You can do anything."

- At a rally in 2024, Trump declared, "I am going to do it, whether the women like it or not," in reference to protecting women. He added, "I am the President. I want to protect the women of our country. ... I am going to do it, whether the women like it or not."

These remarks exemplify a persistent association between traditional masculinity, control, and a disregard for female autonomy. For some men, aligning with this rhetoric can feel like a way to assert their masculine identity. This phenomenon reflects the adage: "The enemy of my enemy is my friend." If men feel insecure or rejected by women, figures who echo their frustrations may seem like allies, reinforcing toxic patterns rather than addressing underlying fears or vulnerabilities. The 2024 U.S. Presidential election brought overt misogyny into political discourse, with Trump's campaign promoting a vision of male dominance that relegated women to subservient roles. This is again the hamster wheel of perceived or even measurable success via being macho, such that being macho is needed to have that success.

Voting as a test of manhood

Electoral analyses reveal notable voting patterns among male demographics, particularly regarding perceptions of masculinity.

- **General male voting trends**

    In the 2024 election, male voters favored Donald Trump over Kamala Harris by margins ranging from 10 to 13 percentage points. Men without a college degree supported Trump by a 22-point margin, while white men favored him by 20 to 23 points. Among white men without a college degree, the preference for Trump widened to a staggering 38-40 point margin. (Cooper, R. (2024). *Democrats' Disastrous Gender Politics*. Compact Magazine.)

- **Young male voters**

    A significant shift occurred among young male voters aged 18 to 29. In 2020, this group supported Joe Biden by 15 points; however, in 2024, they favored Donald Trump by 14 points, marking a 29-point swing in a single election cycle. (Cooper, R. (2024). Democrats '*Disastrous Gender Politics*. Compact Magazine.)

Trump's statements, though framed as political rhetoric, were less about policy and more about amplifying toxic masculinity, using dominance and provocation to appeal to disaffected men. His approach successfully galvanized like-minded individuals by exploiting their fears and frustrations, a strategy reflected in voting trends. Statistics show a growing shift among male voters, particularly younger and non-college-educated men, toward candidates like Trump and Vance, whose personas reinforce traditional or rigid masculinity ideals.

For many men, this alignment is not about political ideology but fear of rejection, fear of inadequacy, and fear of vulnerability. It also allows young men to feel like they're choosing a side that exhibits strength and power. Figures like Trump offer them a sense of strength through a shared adversary — women. Elliot Rodger's tragic example shows that when men internalize rejection and align themselves with rhetoric that fuels anger and resentment, it can spiral into catastrophic consequences. Rodger's manifesto revealed how deeply unchecked cultural norms around male dominance and emotional isolation can reinforce toxic masculinity.

This is not about who is right or wrong in politics. It is about how masculinity has become a political tool; one that divides men instead of helping them. Whether it is Trump's brash dominance or Biden's empathetic leadership, each version of masculinity is held up as "the right way to be a man." However, masculinity is not a campaign

Understanding the Problem

slogan. Moreover, it sure as hell should not be something we vote on. Yet we do.

Masculinity and mental health – the quiet epidemic

You see it everywhere: the father who refuses to hug his son because he does not want him to "get soft," the father that does not hug his son for his own fear of vulnerability, the teenager who hides his fear and anxiety behind aggression, and the man who works 80 hours a week because he believes his worth is tied to his paycheck. These examples are not just anecdotal; they reflect a deeply ingrained cultural belief system.

Just like Elliot Rodger's tragedy, the emotional effects on young men's trajectory appear downward.

- Men account for 79% of all suicides, dying by suicide at a rate four times higher than women. (Heads Up Guys)

- Men die due to alcohol-related causes at a rate of 62,000 annually, compared to 26,000 for women. (National Institute of Mental Health)

- Additionally, men are two to three times more likely to misuse drugs than women. (National Institute of Mental Health)

There is also a troubling rise in Body Dysmorphia Disorder (BDD) among young men, driven by reinforced ideals of masculinity from TV shows, social media influencers, and Hollywood actors. Studies indicate an increasing proportion of men with BDD, now exceeding women. In some instances, this is compounded by a lack of diagnosis and understanding. (American Psychological Association (APA), "The Effects of Media Exposure on Male Body Image," available at apa.org.)

Over the past two decades, there has been a significant increase in the enrollment of women in law and medical schools. In the early 2000s, women comprised approximately 45% of law school students; by 2020, that number had risen to over 54%. Similarly, in medical schools, female enrollment increased from about 46% in 2000 to nearly 52% in 2020. These trends indicate a shift towards greater gender parity in professional education. (American Bar Association (ABA), "Profile of Legal Profession," available at americanbar.org, Association of American Medical Colleges (AAMC), "2022 Medical School Enrollment by Gender," available at aamc.org.)

This section has not been added with the intent to promote competition between men and women but rather to show the factual stagnation of men in these areas.

> *What is the cause of young women outpacing young men in higher educational fields, like law and medicine? Have women changed and improved, or is this another statistic that coincides with the downward trends young men face today?*

Toxic masculinity does not just hurt men; it isolates them. Research indicates that adherence to traditional masculine norms, often referred to as "toxic masculinity," can lead to social isolation among men. Notable studies include:

- **Hegemonic Masculinity and Social Isolation**

A Michigan State University Study by sociologists found that men who endorse hegemonic ideals of masculinity, such as toughness, self-reliance, and emotional suppression, are more likely to become socially isolated as they age. Moreover, it showed that this isolation negatively impacts their health, well-being, and overall happiness. It seems the statistics about this being a toxic masculinity issue are correct.

The study highlights how traditional gender norms discourage men from seeking emotional support, leading to greater loneliness and mental health struggles. (Vandello, J. A., & Bosson, J. K. (2020). *Toxic Masculinity is Unsafe Even for Men*. Michigan State University Research Report.)

- **Masculinity Norms and Loneliness**

A review published in Psychology of Men & Masculinities examines traditional masculinity norms with loneliness and social connectedness among men in Western cultures. The review found that emphasizing independence and emotional stoicism increases men's vulnerability to loneliness and hinders the development of meaningful relationships. (Seidler, Z. E., Dawes, G. M., Rice, S. M., Oliffe, J. L., & Dhillon, H. M. (2020). *The Role of Masculinity in Men's Help-Seeking for Depression: A Systematic Review.* Psychology of Men & Masculinities, 21(2), 205-218.)

A trait, masculinity, being portrayed as a benefit for men, is part of the harm.

- **Masculinity, Social Connectedness, and Mental Health:**

An article in the *American Journal of Men's Health* explored how traditional masculine behaviors impact men's ability to seek social support. The findings indicate that men who rigidly conform to traditional masculinity definitions struggle to form deep social connections, which then negatively affects their mental health and contributes to increased levels of stress, anxiety, and depression. (Mahalik, J. R., Burns, S. M., & Syzdek, M. (2019). *Social Connectedness, Masculinity Ideology, and Mental Health in Men.* American Journal of Men's Health, 13(5), 1557988319873537.)

These studies collectively highlight how rigid adherence to traditional masculine norms by suppressing their emotions can lead to social isolation, adversely affecting men's mental health issues, from depression to anxiety, which, in turn, can lead them to feel unable to ask for help. The pressure to conform leads to strained relationships, feelings of inadequacy, and, in some cases, dangerous behaviors like substance abuse or violence, as the statistics in this chapter have shown.

From pressure to presence – my personal reckoning

Looking back on my own life, I can see how deeply these beliefs shaped me. My father would say, "David, do not cry. Real men do not cry." My brother and friends echoed the same refrain: "David, you're too sensitive. Stop that." I vividly remember moments when the pressure felt unbearable, the weight of conflicting emotions pulling me in opposite directions. Should I conform to their expectations, suppressing what I knew in my heart? Or should I stay true to what truly mattered to me? More often than not, confusion and fear won, and I found myself going along with the flow, burying my emotions and silencing my inner voice. Each time I did, it felt like I was chipping away at pieces of myself I could never get back.

I was dreadfully afraid of rejection by women and of failure, or not meeting the standards of societal success. Much of my first book, The Imperative Habit, discussed this fear at length. Am I alone in this thinking?

What I was also most terrified of was what other men, women, family, and friends would think of me if I didn't conform to societal expectations of being a "Real Man". What would I think of myself? Could I be okay departing from what I felt was the norm, being something so different, sensitive, and non-masculine? This led to behaviors that didn't promote my growth, but hindered it. I acted to meet standards rather than being myself, suppressing feelings, emotions, ideas, wants, desires, and dreams.

Looking back on my life through the lens of a healthier form of masculinity, I can see how many of my choices were driven by the fear of feeling inadequate, of being seen as less, and by the relentless pursuit of what I thought success should look like. So many of my efforts were motivated by those fears and desires rather than by the authentic joy and life directions my heart truly yearned for. It took me years to realize how many opportunities I'd missed by chasing society's standards of being a "real man" instead of following my most heartfelt intentions. I often wonder about the moments of love I passed by, and what they could have brought to my life, and where they might have led me. These missed opportunities touched every part of my world: my work, my personal and romantic relationships, and even my family.

I know feeling vulnerable often feels like weakness. We fear what others might think of us, worrying that sharing our struggles will strip us of the title of "real man." Perhaps, based on our own internalized ideals, we wouldn't even call ourselves that. The thought of exposing those fears can feel unbearable. Yet, it is that act of strength to be vulnerable, to share the weakness that needs to be shared to grow and improve, that is the basis for true growth and real masculinity.

Portraying the strength to be weak in the face of fear is transformative.

I am not religious, nor do I profess to be a Christian. However, the Bible and Jesus Christ's teachings can be profound. St. Paul's words to the Lord in 2 Corinthians 12:9 resonate deeply: My strength is made perfect by my weakness. Through our vulnerability, we uncover the greatest opportunities for growth, not just as human beings but as real men.

Research shows that men who express vulnerability cultivate deeper and more meaningful connections. Vulnerability is not a weakness; it's the foundation of authenticity. Dr. Brené Brown, a leading researcher on shame and vulnerability, captures this beautifully: "Vulnerability is not about winning or losing. It's having the courage to show up when you can't control the outcome." This is where this book pivots to authenticity. The ultimate goal is to live as your authentic self. Learning to embrace this courage transformed how I connected with others. It shifted my focus from proving my worth to living authentically. Needless to say, it seems Dr. Brené Brown agrees with St. Paul's words.

Comments From Brad Kearns

This chapter has some seriously disturbing and heavy information. As I read it, I realized I was creating an affirmation in my mind that this stuff was important to learn, but not really about me. I never got into any of that macho man or pickup artist stuff. I've never been mistaken for an alpha male.

After all, I was usually the smallest and youngest kid in my grade, so I trended more toward class clown. I became a distance runner, not the football player or basketball star I dreamed of being. I don't think I engage in much emotional suppression. I don't think I'm swayed at all by advertising messages targeting males. I don't think I put on masks of masculinity.

Blah, blah blah, can you see where I'm going yet? That's right, masks and deceptions can take on different forms. One of them can be how you fool yourself - thinking you're above the fray because the graphic, in-your-face examples don't apply to you. During the reading, I realized that the story I was cooking up in my head - that the chapter wasn't relevant to me - was a form of masking up! As you continue to read, strive to keep an open mind and willingness to learn, even if the information and anecdotes don't seem to hit your bullseye.

Chapter 1: Wrap up

This chapter isn't about blaming men for buying into these cultural myths; it's about understanding how deeply ingrained they are in society and the harm they cause. By acknowledging the problem, we can rewrite the narrative for a healthier, more authentic version of masculinity and ourselves. Authenticity is the first rebellion.

A call to awareness

Before moving to Chapter 2, I challenge you to do this:

Tonight, take just five minutes before you fall asleep. Ask yourself:

- Where today did I feel the pressure to perform, to compete, or to hide how I was really feeling?

- Where did I adjust myself, even subtly, to fit someone else's image of a "real man"?

Write down whatever comes up. No edits. No judgment. Just awareness. Awareness is the first crack in the armor. You can't fix a script you don't even realize you're reading.

This small act of awareness is not just a journal entry; it's your first rebellion against a broken story. It's the first breath of a life that belongs to you, not the world's expectations.

I spent years chasing an idea of masculinity that wasn't mine. I know I'm not alone. The question is: *Are you ready to stop pretending and start defining masculinity for yourself?*

(If we don't, someone else will do it for us.)

Next chapter

In Chapter two, we'll dive deeper into the "problem" of the Real Man paradigm, examining the root of the problem more closely. As Einstein said, "If I had an hour to solve a problem, I would spend 55 minutes thinking about the problem and five minutes thinking about solutions."

Chapter 2:

Why We Need a New Definition of Masculinity

As discussed in Chapter 1, traditional masculinity operates not only on outdated principles—dominance, suppression of emotions, and an unrelenting focus on achievement—but also on traits that differ from culture to culture, state to state, city to city, and even person to person or woman/man to man. While these traits may have served a purpose for men in the past, they are ill-equipped for the complexities of the transfer rate of information in the modern era. The rate at which information moves and the pace of socio-economic shifts across regions has never been faster. Socialized masculinity traits have not kept up with modern life. It is akin to advances in military technology without adapting to new military tactics. I call this the cost of stagnation.

In the late 19th century, for example, the technological advancement of the machine gun changed warfare forever. It could fire hundreds of rounds per minute, turning battlefields into more efficient killing zones. Yet, when World War I began in 1914, military tactics had not changed for over a century! Generals, trained in the traditions of Napoleonic warfare, still sent soldiers to fight in tight, orderly rows, marching into enemy fire as if they were still facing muskets, rather than machine guns.

The result was slaughter. Men advanced shoulder-to-shoulder, only to be mowed down in waves by relentless machine gun fire. At battles like the 1916 Somme offensive, tens of thousands fell in a single day, their lives wasted in attacks that gained no ground. The machine gun did not discriminate, cutting down the brave, the fearful, the young, and the old alike.

It took years of unimaginable bloodshed before armies adapted to modern technology. Why? By the time tactics were changed, millions had senselessly died not because the machine gun was unstoppable, but because people failed to see that the old ways of war were obsolete. This is the cost of stagnation.

When you consider what's happening to young men today, just in an emotional and psychological form, it's clear that while there have been centuries of human advancements, the traditional role of masculinity, now called "toxic," has remained the same.

This isn't about social awkwardness or out-of-touch fashion. These outdated tactics are leading to disconnection, discontent, and emotional death.

Even the most popular and current masculinity books seem to miss the core problem. In fact, I don't know of one book, class, blog, or podcast that has accurately deciphered the solution to men's masculinity problems in today's society. One so-called bestseller even created twelve masculine archetypes! And men are supposed to try to put themselves into one? To me, rather than adding clarity, an addition of new archetype only creates four times the confusion of traditional archetype mask-wearing.

A primary reason is that the old model and corresponding masculinity traits are still heavily tied to a more biological or physiological drive. Think of it more like the Darwinian "survival of the fittest." When Darwin wrote his thesis on evolution, he truly meant "fittest". He meant that the biggest gorilla was the fittest, or the fastest cheetah was the fittest. He meant it as a localized competition between males to dominate and create the best offspring — and rightfully so.

What is "the fittest" today? An influencer? Someone with money? Someone with abs? Someone who has both? Someone who dresses nicely, has a nice car, and can cook Beef Wellington? Today, even the idea of "being on top" has lost meaning. The whole system of social fitness is fragmented. We're still running two-million-year-old outdated biological software in a society that requires spiritual hardware.

But to what extent? What exactly needs to change?

As we can see, the definition of "fittest" in 2025 is a slippery slope. Not only does it appear that young men are still attached to outdated Darwinian principles, but they are also looking at how they can match what they view as the "fittest." And, in today's modern life, that's a wide range of traits. What we're finding is that men are constantly shape-shifting and trying on new personas in an endless loop of social trial-and-error. Andrew Tate is one example, but he's just the tip of the iceberg.

Today, young men cycle through a revolving door of personas: the "Sigma Male" who disengages from society to "be his own boss," the hustle culture guru who preaches working until you drop (think Gary Vee), or the fitness influencer who equates self-worth with muscle mass. Each persona starts with promises of success, but none delivers lasting fulfillment. Even the so-called "woke" updates are still just upgraded masks. The whole model has expired.

What happens when people try to pretend to be something they're not? They're fake! They're not themselves. They have a veneer. How sustainable do you think it is to pretend to be something or someone else? It typically lasts only as long as it is successful. If it's not successful, there's a general abandonment of the persona, while one looks to adopt a new persona, believing this one might work. What is the cost of stagnation in this model? When the cycle of false identity continues with no lasting results, it leads to depression, isolation, confusion, and discontent. These are all symptoms that I believe contribute to the downward spiral we're seeing in the statistics around men.

As Professor Scott Galloway has said publicly on the The Gray Area podcast[1], where Sean Illing interviewed Scott Galloway, on December 16, 2024:

> "No group has fallen faster and farther than young men in America. Four out of five suicides are men. One in three men under 30 have girlfriends, yet two out of three girls under 30 have boyfriends... because women under 30 are dating men over 30 who are economically and emotionally more viable than men under 30."

Don't get me wrong. Darwin was right. Animals do and will propagate based on the survival of the fittest. And that's where the difficulty lies. We're still animals. But we're also Homo sapiens. We are thinking cognitive animals who no longer live in constant survival mode.

We've retained the DNA, hormones, and neurotransmitters from 70,000 years ago, and those primal systems are still running in us today. We still have urges to dominate, impress, and survive. The thoughts, ideas, and rationalizations of men to emulate the personas of other successful men are the outdated tactics of the Napoleonic era, wherein modern life is the proverbial machine gun, mowing young men down statistically, mentally, emotionally, and financially. And yet, young men think the way to beat the machine gun is to stay the course of traditional masculinity and just assume we're not doing it right. The problem is that we haven't learned how to hold those urges at bay or how to use them consciously in modern society.

That's where men are losing today. And that's why we must shift to a new model.

We need to stop being slaves to our outdated biological urges or animalistic instincts and start using our power to make real choices about our actions.

Women face similar challenges, but they've been conditioned to process their discontent differently. While men often mask weakness with performance, women are more likely to seek support. The masculine traits that create the problem of emotional suppression, stoicism, and dominance also perpetuate it by reinforcing a false veneer of strength. This conditioning is generational, passed down, and rarely questioned.

One in five men under 30 still lives at home, while single women now own more homes than single men (Galloway, 2024). When struggling, women tend to reach out; men tend to retreat. Research confirms that

References

1. Vox Media

women maintain more intimate support networks (Taylor et al., 2000), while men are less likely to seek help, and therefore face increased isolation and worsening mental health (Seidler et al., 2016).

For men today, trying to adopt a successful persona is a guessing game. However, there's one constant in traditional masculinity: the need to portray strength. To clarify, this requirement in today's society is not to legitimately be strong, but simply just to look strong. We mistakenly think this performance is what will help us find connection, belonging, or emotional safety. It has never been easier to portray something that isn't in today's media platforms.

Is the need for change not yet obvious? Picture this: you're standing in line like a soldier from the Napoleonic era, shoulder to shoulder with other men, walking into the machine gun of modern life still believing brute stoicism will protect you.

It won't.

So, what's the alternative? We get real. We get vulnerable.

Vulnerability is the first step toward real strength — toward authenticity — but we've been taught to equate it with weakness. That lie traps men in emotional stagnation, which turns into anger, anxiety, withdrawal, and disconnection. We stay stuck, misunderstood, and isolated.

As I said in Chapter 1, to express emotion, to admit weakness, takes strength. The courage to show your naked truth takes more power than hiding it ever will. When vulnerability becomes a daily habit, it transforms into invulnerability. That's real strength.

I've lived on both sides of the mask. The turning point came when my life collapsed — my company, my marriage, my sense of identity. It was all self-inflicted. I'd stayed too long in an emotionally abusive relationship, chasing the illusion of being "the fittest". I wore the mask because I feared what being divorced would mean — not to me, but to society. And that fear kept me stuck for years. That was the cost of stagnation.

I told myself I was winning, providing, succeeding, staying "strong", but really, I was suffocating. And when I began to compute the cost of leaving, I realized the mask wasn't just uncomfortable. It was killing me.

When my company began to dissolve, a man named Todd, who was buying parts of the business, mocked me: "what kind of man are you? You can't even make payroll." It crushed me. But instead of fighting back, I said, "I get it. Thanks for your opinion." That was a defining moment. I didn't need to be the bigger gorilla. I didn't need to win. I just needed to start climbing out.

Was I any less of a man for walking away from a toxic marriage? Or was that my first real act of manhood? The answer doesn't matter. We need to stop asking the question.

Here's what did matter: I reminded myself that vulnerability leads to strength. I reminded myself I'm not defined by failure or judgment. I got myself here, and I could get myself out. That was my first real step toward becoming an Omega Man.

If you've ever felt like that — lost, ashamed, uncertain — know this: you have two choices.

> **Option #1:** Double down. Pick a new persona, a new mask. Maybe it's something you saw on Instagram, in a boardroom, or on a stage. Maybe it looks like strength. But it's not sustainable.

> **Option #2:** Drop the act. Accept that the mask doesn't work. Choose a new definition of masculinity — one that isn't driven by biology or bravado, but by presence. This is Joseph Campbell's hero's journey. And the call to adventure? It's right here.

Option #1 leads to burnout, disconnection, and constant reinvention. Option #2 leads to clarity, connection, and a life that feels real.

Embracing vulnerability isn't a moral pitch; it's survival in the modern world. Studies show men who practice it have stronger relationships, greater fulfillment, and deeper emotional stability (Karney & Bradbury, 1995; Fineman, 2008; TIME, 2024).

This is not just about feeling better; it's about living better.

A new definition of masculinity must center on vulnerability and emotional intelligence, not as weaknesses, but as the new pillars of real strength. It's about admitting failure without shame. Facing discomfort without denial. Embracing humanity without armor. Vulnerability becomes the bridge to real connection, the compass for grounded action, and the tool for resilience.

It's not about rejecting masculinity. It's about redefining it. One rooted in authenticity over performance, connection over dominance, and growth over image. This model doesn't ask you to become someone else. It asks you to become yourself.

Why does authenticity matter? Because the deeper we live in truth, the more we cut through the noise of insecurity, trauma, and societal programming which will reduce the drive to wear a mask.

Authenticity is the sword that slays our inner demons: inadequacy, social anxiety, and fear of judgment. It begins by shedding the outer veneer — the one society expects — and ends with awakening the Self.

In spiritual language, "self" with a lowercase "s" is your ego, your survival mask. "Self" with a capital "S" is who you truly are, beneath the fear and performance. That's what Einstein meant when he said:

> *"The true value of a human being can be found in the degree to which he has attained liberation from the self."*

The spiritual journey is about liberating yourself from the false self. That's what this book is inviting you to do.

And let's be clear. Authenticity isn't just a lifestyle brand. It's the foundation for meaning, purpose, and peace. When men drop the performance and accept their truth, everything changes. Their relationships deepen. Their voice returns. Their life begins.

This is still early in the book — still just Chapter 2 — but this is the chapter where you start to see that there is another way.

I wore the mask of traditional masculinity for years, thinking that if I stayed strong, didn't flinch, and didn't break, I'd be seen as worthy. But when I finally dropped the act and let myself see who I was, flaws and all, I found a different kind of strength. Not loud. Not performative. Just real. Solid. Quiet. And unshakable.

This isn't theory. This chapter isn't just an analysis. It's an invitation to stop performing and start becoming. Drop the roles. Strip back the layers. Live as the man you were meant to be before the world told you who you had to become.

Chapter 2: The problem wrap

The problem isn't that you're broken. The problem is that you're playing by rules that were designed for survival, not fulfillment. And you're waking up to that truth, which means you're already ahead of the game.

Next chapter

In the next chapter, we'll dive deeper into the role of fear the invisible force that keeps us chained to outdated beliefs and behaviors and tied to stagnation. We'll explore how fear shapes our instincts, how it drives us to cling to old tactics even when they no longer serve us, and how we can begin to replace those instincts with intentionality. The journey to a new masculinity isn't just about letting go of the past; it's about building a future where we respond to life not out of fear, but out of purpose. It's not just theoretical; it's life and death.

Are you ready to take the first step?

Comments From Brad Kearns

That's a pretty disturbing comparison between World War I machine guns and flawed and dated traditional notions of masculinity! But it makes sense. We're definitely stuck in survival of the fittest mode. We're operating with 70,000-year-old software.

I like how Dave positions the message that we need to realize and acknowledge how we are using dated software, and that we can't just snap our fingers and turn it off. That's a mistake that I see in a lot of pop psychology expert recommendations. Here, put on this "woke-update" mask and you will be cool. This is kinda what playah's do in the dating world. They project a stylized persona to achieve an outcome, but of course it's an act that wears off and often leads to dysfunction and heartbreak.

One point of clarity I want to emphasize here: The idea is to stop performing and become vulnerable, while also still acknowledging the powerful influence of your inherent biological programming. John Gray details this idea beautifully in his book, Beyond Mars and Venus. We have powerful hard-wired biological drives that we can't ignore (that would be wearing a mask!), and these drives and hormonal processes have a strong influence in our behaviors, especially our love relationships.

As Dave mentions, males tend to retreat when they struggle, while females tend to reach out and seek connection. In general (and not to offend woke readers), males are biologically wired to solve problems, conquer challenges, and so forth. We have to realize it's not our inclination to reach out and connect and discuss issues at length, but that we can benefit from stepping up and doing so. We are not naturally inclined to be vulnerable (as might be the case with inherent female biological wiring to nurture and connect), but that we can benefit from stepping up and doing so.

Know that it's gonna be a challenge to swim upstream against your biological programming, but that you can do it! That's a big difference from pretending that you're not swimming upstream, you know? We're still animals with primitive programming running in the background, but we can overwrite with new code by maintaining heightened awareness.

Chapter 3:

Fear —The Hidden Driver of Masculinity

"Attorney and law professor Mark Lemley has publicly severed ties with Meta, the parent company of Facebook and Instagram, citing CEO Mark Zuckerberg's 'descent into toxic masculinity and Neo-Nazi madness.'"

> The decision announced on LinkedIn comes amidst a whirlwind of controversial changes at Meta ... Zuckerberg's recent comments on Joe Rogan's podcast, where he advocated for more 'masculine energy' in corporate culture, have only fueled the controversy. The CEO's political pivot towards former President Donald Trump, including a $1 million donation to Trump's inauguration fund, marks a stark departure from his earlier criticisms of Trump's rhetoric."[1]

At the core of traditional masculinity lies fear — the fear of being seen as weak; the fear of not conforming; the fear of failure; and the fear of not measuring up to societal expectations. However, more importantly, perhaps most insidiously, the fear of being in a situation evokes fear.

Fear is afraid of itself. It is a self-reinforcing loop, doing everything in its power to keep us from confronting it directly.

The driver?

References

1. Vaidehi Mehta, Esq. | Last updated on January 27, 2025

Our DNA and the drive to be the Darwinian "fittest".

From a Darwinian perspective, this is helpful for an organism. Fear kept early humans alive. It told them to run from predators or avoid dangerous situations, ensuring survival. This instinct served a critical purpose in an environment where daily life was fraught with immediate, life-threatening risks.

Nevertheless, here is the key: while our environments have evolved dramatically, our hormonal and neurotransmitter responses to fear essentially remain the same. The chemicals that surged through our ancestors' veins as they fled sabre-toothed tigers are the same ones coursing through Mark Zuckerberg's body when deciding his political allegiance or managing public scrutiny.

Mark Zuckerberg and the "squirrel nut theory"

For Zuckerberg, and in the complexities of his life, it's possible his decision-making is influenced more by primal patterns than by conscious, value-driven reasoning — like the "fight or flight" impulse. The stakes in his world may not involve literal survival, but the expression of these primal instincts still echoes in high-pressure moments. In 2020, this manifested as support for Biden. By 2024, it had flipped to supporting Trump. Neither choice was inherently right or wrong, but it did underscore something deeper — is this an example of reactive survival-mode thinking, or a strategic calculation? Maybe both. But it's a compelling lens through which to examine how even the most powerful among us might still be subtly governed by fear.

Fight or flight, while effective for ensuring survival in our evolutionary past, is neither sustainable nor sufficient for navigating the nuanced challenges of modern life. Zuckerberg's decisions, though complex on the surface, seem rooted in a reactive mode rather than something greater, something more aligned with higher awareness. What would happen if his choices extended beyond instinctual survival? Could they become something more sustainable, enlightened, and akin to the expansive perspective that Einstein alluded to in his famous quote about solving problems from a higher level of consciousness?

This is where the "Squirrel Nut Theory" comes in. A squirrel hoards nuts instinctively, driven by fear of scarcity. Even when its burrow is overflowing, it continues to gather more, unable to recognize that it already has enough. Humans, despite our higher cognition, often behave in similar ways. Even someone as wealthy and influential as Zuckerberg can remain trapped in this instinctual cycle, driven by fear rather than purpose.

This thought brings me, in a way, to a quote I'm fond of: *"Where love rules, there is no will to power; and where power predominates, love is lacking."* — Carl Jung

With that in mind, here is the question: Haven't we, as humans, transcended the animal kingdom? Shouldn't we be able to rise above these primal instincts?

The unfortunate answer is 'not always'. Fear still governs many of our decisions, often without our conscious awareness.

Instinctual behaviors: Dominance and peacocking

Instinctually, males must express dominance over other males, signaling they should back down and leave a particular female for their selection. This behavior ties directly to the survival-of-the-fittest framework, where strength and dominance determine mating opportunities. Further, males must "peacock" to females to display their fitness and attract attention.

Instinctually, a man showing vulnerability is a fast pass to displaying "least fit for survival" to other men and women. In the animal kingdom, males need to show off their feathers, not just to attract females but to assert dominance over other males. A peacock's vibrant feathers, a stag's antlers, or a lion's mane all serve the same purpose: to signal strength, fitness, and superiority.

This behavior may manifest in less obvious ways for humans, but the instinct remains. Men might flaunt wealth, physical prowess, or social status as a way of peacocking in both social and romantic contexts. This instinctual drive to demonstrate fitness persists, even when it conflicts with the complexities of modern society.

The challenge, however, is that this deeply-ingrained behavior often creates barriers to authentic connection and personal growth. While vulnerability might feel like signaling weakness or "least fit for survival," in truth, it's the opposite. Vulnerability requires immense courage, making it a sign of strength, not weakness. Yet, fear convinces us otherwise, urging us to continue "peacocking," even when it limits our ability to build meaningful relationships and achieve personal fulfillment.

How fear rationalizes behaviors

Fear has an insidious way of rationalizing our actions. It tricks us into believing that conforming to societal expectations is the only path to safety and success. From an early age, boys are taught to avoid vulnerability at all costs. To show vulnerability, they are told, is to invite humiliation, inadequacy, or even failure. This conditioning plants the seeds of fear that grow into the rigid, defensive behaviors associated with toxic masculinity.

This brings us to another animal analogy: herd survival. In the wild, animals that blend in with their herd are less likely to attract predators. A zebra that matches the patterns of its group has a better chance of survival than one that stands out. Imagine if one zebra decided to jump and dance, drawing attention to itself. It would immediately become a target.

Similarly, societal norms teach men to blend in by conforming to rigid roles. While humans have the capacity for individuality, fear often compels us to behave like herd animals to varying degrees. We fear that standing out by showing vulnerability or defying masculine norms will make us targets for judgment or rejection.

I once spoke with a man who told me he'd never cried in front of his kids. Not once. Not even when his own father died. Jason, who was 38 at the time and a father of two, looked to me for help in changing some aspects of his life.

"I thought that was strength," he said. "I thought staying composed was what made me a man."

But then, one evening, his 8-year-old son looked up at him and asked, "Dad... do men cry?"

That moment hit Jason harder than anything he'd faced before. Not because he didn't know the answer, but because the question revealed what he'd been teaching his son. He didn't like the lesson.

"I wasn't protecting my kids," he told me later, after our work. "I was protecting my fear. I was afraid to be seen." Jason wanted to be the best father he could; that drive helped him work on his spiritual awareness and spiritual behavior.

Jason wasn't alone. Most men wear armor that looks like strength but is really just a shield for fear. Fear of being exposed. Fear of being judged. Fear of being honest about how much we feel.

Do you now see?

Can you now see the role fear plays in influencing men's decisions? Can you see that we prioritize safety by behaving in conformity over risk and authenticity? Fear of failure might prevent a man from pursuing his passions, while fear of rejection might keep him from expressing his true feelings. These fear-based decisions limit personal growth and create a sense of dissatisfaction and unfulfilled potential.

Societal impacts: Living with fear

When men live with fear, the impacts ripple outward. I'm not talking about the kind of fear that may immediately rise to mind — like hiding in a closet, afraid a burglar has entered your house — but the kind of fear I've been talking about throughout this book. Fear of vulnerability. Fear of non-conformity. Fear of not winning. And, most importantly, the subconscious fear of not being the "fittest" and not surviving as robustly as other males at the proverbial watering hole.

Fear is not just an individual burden. When young men live with these deeply ingrained fears, the effects spread to families, workplaces, and communities. Families suffer from distant fathers, emotionally unavailable partners, and fractured relationships. Workplaces lose out on empathetic leaders and collaborative environments. Society as a whole bears the burden of untreated mental health issues, toxic behaviors, and the compounding impacts of rigid masculinity. The societal cost of clinging to outdated ideals of masculinity is immense and unsustainable.

A comprehensive study titled *"The Cost of the Man Box"* examined the economic impacts of harmful masculine stereotypes in the United States. The study found that men who internalize rigid gender norms are more likely to engage in risky behaviors such as excessive drinking and reckless driving. These behaviors lead to significant economic costs, including healthcare expenses, loss of productivity, harm to interpersonal relationships, and damage to personal health. The study concluded that challenging and changing these outdated ideals could result in substantial economic and social benefits (Equimundo, 2021).

Yet, despite this data, these behaviors continue to persist, often going unchecked, leading to further harm and perpetuation of toxic cycles.

Key data on masculinity and societal impacts

Here are some stark statistics that highlight the profound societal and personal impacts of these outdated masculine norms:

- **Mental health:** A survey by the youth mental health charity Stem4 found that 37% of boys and young men aged 14 to 21 were experiencing mental health difficulties. Of these, 51% had not spoken to anyone about their struggles. The most common issues reported were stress (47%), anxiety (27%), and depression or low mood (33%) (Stem4, 2021).

- **Avoidance of help:** The same survey revealed that 46% of respondents would not ask for help for problems causing them distress, even if the situation became severe. Reasons included not having the courage (36%), not wanting to make a fuss (32%), feeling weak or ashamed (30%), and concerns about appearing less masculine (14%) (Stem4, 2021).

- **Substance abuse:** Men adhering to traditional masculine norms are more likely to engage in risky behaviors, including increased substance and alcohol use. Significantly more men than women died from opioid overdoses as of 2018 (Very well Mind, 2023).

- **Premature mortality:** In the Americas, one in five men will not reach the age of 50, with issues related to toxic masculinity contributing to this statistic. Men also live almost six years less than women, with social constructs around masculinity playing a significant role (Pan American Health Organization, 2019).

- **Aggression and violence:** Toxic masculinity is linked to increased aggression and the perpetuation of sexism, homophobia, and other forms of discrimination. These behaviors harm interpersonal relationships and contribute to societal issues such as domestic violence and gender inequality (Health, 2023).

- **Education gaps**: Recent exam results in Scotland show a widening performance gap between boys and girls, with girls achieving higher grades. Experts point to behavioral differences and a lack of positive male role models as contributing factors, suggesting that aspects of toxic masculinity may hinder boys' academic performance (The Times, 2023).

- **Workplace safety:** Men are more likely to engage in dangerous occupations and are less likely to seek help for health issues, leading to higher rates of workplace injuries and fatalities. In the United States, men account for 92% of workplace deaths (The Australian, 2023).

Adherence to harmful masculine stereotypes also contributes to increased rates of binge drinking and traffic accidents among men. A study by Equimundo and Axe estimated that eliminating these harmful norms could save the U.S. economy approximately $15.7 billion annually, with $181 million attributed to binge drinking and $7.3 billion to traffic accidents (Equimundo, 2021).

Are you ready to stop being a negative statistic?

Conclusion to "the problem"

To summarize, Part I of this book, The Problem, starts and stops with young men's major disconnect with their higher selves.

Someone once told me the definition of hell:

> *"The last day you have on earth, the person you became will meet the person you could have become."*

This concept aligns perfectly with Leo Tolstoy's The Death of Ivan Ilyich, wherein Ivan, on his deathbed, says:

> *"What if I lived my entire life wrong?"*

It is a substantial challenge to reach or even live a portion of your life as your highest self, but why not try? Not trying to live your best life, or at least striving toward the highest version of yourself, is what actually causes this problem for men.

The real travesty is that young men remain trapped in a downward cycle of stagnation — the squirrel nut theory in action, driven by the need to stay "Neanderthalic" rather than evolving into enlightened Homo Sapiens. To connect with your highest self means departing from false versions of yourself. It means recognizing when you are "acting," "pretending," "mimicking," or "peacocking" in the hopes of gaining approval. And above all, it means working toward stopping those behaviors.

Spiritual awareness

A central aspect of this book will be for men to strive toward their highest selves. For that, spiritual behaviors will be required. Before diving into what that entails in Part II, let's define Spiritual Awareness for the purpose of this book.

Imagine running for exercise. As you run harder and longer, your muscles begin to provide biological feedback to your brain. Lactic acid builds up, your legs grow heavy, and your heart rate and lung capacity strain under the exertion. Fatigue sets in, and your body urgently sends this biological feedback to your brain: "Stop."

But then, something remarkable happens. Another voice in your mind counters: "Keep going. This is where champions are made." This second voice speaks beyond your biological feedback and urges you to push past the discomfort.

This is the definition of spirituality for this book: a voice that speaks beyond the biological feedback of survivability. Spiritual awareness is being aware of the contradiction between your body's plea to stop and your spirit's call to persevere. Acting on that voice, despite the biological feedback, is spiritual behavior.

The problem is that few people realize this same spiritual awareness and behavior must be applied to all aspects of life, not just athletics. It must empower men to overcome fear, embrace vulnerability, and resist the urge to conform to societal norms. Mostly, so if the are toxic.

Personal reflection

In my journey, fear was a constant companion. I was afraid of failing, of being judged, and, most of all, of being truly seen. But I had no idea I could use my strengths in athletics to keep fear at bay. It was no different than what I'd done in sports my whole life when facing physical fatigue.

Looking back now, I see how beating social norms was elusive. And now, how much more powerful emotional feedback was than physical feedback. Emotional fear, caused by whatever reason, is just a thought; yet those thoughts are powerful. I know now that it's because the brain associates emotional feedback with "not surviving," just like running until exhaustion.

Interestingly enough, emotional thoughts are often coupled with imagination. An active imagination can convert any emotional fear into a powerful, real-life doom-and-gloom scenario, even though that scenario is, ultimately, only a thought.

It wasn't until I began to confront these fears and recognize them as mere thoughts generated from biological feedback that I realized how much they had been controlling my life and my choices. Ultimately, they'd end up leading to many failures. I often think back to sports. What if I'd listened to my body every time it said to stop exercising when I felt tired? I would never have amounted to anything athletically. Why, then, was I listening so intently to the mental chatter tied to the emotional fear that was disguised as conformity, stress, losing out, or not being "good enough"?

Embracing vulnerability in the face of all these thoughts, and then letting go of them, was liberating. I began to see these fears for what they truly were — just like tired legs in a workout. Once I saw them as nothing more than biological feedback, I could let them pass. Doing so allowed me to build deeper relationships, make more meaningful choices, and, above all, live more authentically.

Fear is powerful because it masks itself as truth. But it isn't the truth. It's merely feedback. Just as it is in athletics, this voice can be overridden by something higher.

You may ask yourself, "What does emotional feedback sound like?" or "How do I catch it in the moment?"

Below are likely things one might say, and also hear themselves say:

- What will they think of me?
- I'd better not say that, it might make me look weak.
- I don't want to seem needy.
- Success means never showing pain.
- I'm fine. Just tired.

A call to awareness

This chapter challenges men to examine how fear influences their lives and consider what might be possible if they let it go. By stepping into courage and confronting their fears, men can break free from the constraints of traditional masculinity and discover a more meaningful, empowered way of being.

This journey is not easy, but it is worth it. We can create lives of deeper meaning and fulfillment by choosing courage over fear, authenticity over conformity, and connection over isolation.

Let us stop being squirrels hoarding nuts. Let us be humans choosing purpose.

Reflection: Where in your life are you still hoarding nuts? What fear is beneath that behavior?

Challenge: Name one place this week you'll act from courage instead of conformity.

Comments From Brad Kearns

Dave has introduced me to interesting concepts like the David Hawkins scale, and this chapter provided a great overview of the general idea of evolving to a higher level than animals and pursuing self-mastery. I'm always inspired when talking to Dave about these concepts, or when reading books or listening to podcasts on this subject matter.

One thing I notice that happens to me regularly: my best intentions and awareness of self-mastery skills desert me when I need them the most! Very frustrating. From my study and deep interest in the subject, I know the best way to respond when conversations gets heated; I know the actions and thoughts I should execute to pull me out of a rut; I know about a big picture perspective that I can shift to in a moment to help me escape from whining, complaining, feeling like a victim, or losing control. Am I'm great at giving advice to others when they're struggling (aren't we all?) But...where do my skills go when I'm under pressure?

When things calm down, I'm great with post-mortem analysis, processing the lessons learned, becoming a better person through experience, and so forth. Then, when the next crisis of the mind or situation comes along, there I go again - reverting to fear response or whatever.

Lately, I've been doing a good job of giving myself permission to be imperfect without judgement or negativity. I think judging oneself harshly is part of the rut—you know what I mean? For example, when you feel guilty about something, it's a way of giving yourself permission to repeat the behavior or remain stuck. For example, you've been so busy lately that you haven't called or written grandma. You know how she loves hearing from you, it makes her day! But hey, all that business travel and overflowing inbox, there's no time for everything.

Because you feel guilty, it makes you a good person who loves your grandma and has just been super busy. If you didn't feel guilty, you'd be a selfish, uncaring asshole who can't even lift a finger for an old lady who shuffles to her mail slot every day at the nursing home, hoping there might be a letter from you. That's the game we play with ourselves. Similarly, be wary of that tendency to offer a reflexive apology every time you misbehave or let others down. Instead, try to live your life in such a way that you don't have to apologize for your behavior, nor feel guilty. Granted, heartfelt apologies are certainly appropriate in many occasions, just don't hide behind them, nor behind guilt. Go for it! Cross the rope!

Chapter 3: "The cost of toxic masculinity" wrap

Now you know. The cost is steep. Too steep to ignore. It's not just lost love or missed opportunities; it's lives unraveling from the inside out. But here's the good news: if the old system is failing, that means a new one can be built.

Next chapter

In the next chapter, we'll start sketching the blueprint. What would a new kind of masculinity look like if it does not kill us slowly but makes us more alive?

Vector of Self-Mastery

Moving away from one, towards ten

Before we move into the solutions to dying young as an Alpha and evolving into the Omega Man, here's a framework that may help you understand what I mean when I refer to "authentic masculinity" or "spiritual behavior."

The higher Self is not meant to be a mystical concept. It's not about religion and certainly not some "woo-woo" idea. It's scientific; it's the part of you that exists beyond fear, ego, and societal conditioning. The absence of ego — the ability to be your authentic Self — is a form of spirituality. It means moving beyond instinctual, animalistic behaviors and acting from a place of conscious awareness and higher intention.

Imagine a vector — a straight line. At one end (let's call it zero) is the animal state where humans behave purely on instinct and survival, much like any other creature in the animal kingdom. At the other end (let's call it ten) is the spiritual state, where behavior is fully conscious, intentional, and completely driven by something higher than biological impulses.

Somewhere along that line, humans developed cognition; they stopped reacting purely on instinct and impulse and began making conscious decisions. This shift moved us off zero, leading us toward civilization, refinement, and higher awareness. Moving from zero to one or two is what we began to call "being civilized." This progression — moving more and more out, or away, from zero (or the animal kingdom) — is where we became less animal and more civilized.

I call this progression "The Vector of Self-Mastery." It describes the journey from reactive, survival-based behavior toward conscious, intentional living, from instinct to insight. This first shift, off zero, was the beginning of human intentionality, where our actions were no longer dictated purely by survival instincts. To me, more intentionality means moving further away from the animal kingdom and closer to the spiritual.

As Yuval Noah Harari describes in *Sapiens: A Brief History of Humankind*[1], cognition allows humans to develop complex social structures, language, and problem-solving skills. It's what elevates us above other species that remain bound to their biological instincts.

As humans progressed, they moved further up this scale. At level one or two, early Homo sapiens began developing basic survival tools and hunting in coordinated groups, rather than through brute force alone. By level three or four, humans started determining where to place utensils in a formal dining setting, dressing not just for function but for identity and status, and forming social hierarchies. By levels five and six, humans expressed themselves through art, music, and early religious or philosophical thought, demonstrating their ability to create meaning beyond survival.

As society evolved further, new layers of refinement appeared with communication through written language, the development of structured governance, and even the social etiquette we now take for granted, such as where to place your elbows at the table or how to engage in respectful conversation. These are levels six through seven.

We go up and up the vector, moving toward level ten — the highest level of being civilized, being fully authentic or spiritual. At this stage, a person operates mostly from spirit (opposite of animals) and with the least influence of animalistic urges. This is where one has complete control over impulses, acting not as our primitive instincts demand but as we consciously choose. If we looked at "The Vector of Self-Mastery"

References

1. Yuval Noah Harari

Understanding the Problem

in terms of words, rather than numbers, it would like this: zero -- cognition → ego awareness → spiritual practice → transcendence – ten.

Darwin described evolution as the process of adaptation and survival, where species that best adjusted to their environment thrived. But what happens when survival is no longer the primary driver of our actions? When we evolve past simply reacting to the world and instead choose how to exist within it? That is the essence of moving closer to level ten — the moment we are no longer ruled by biological urges but by our higher awareness. To have the ability to act beyond feedback, like if we continue to run even though our body, mind, and voice tell us to stop. Harking back to the working out example I used in Chapter 3, when you exercise, your body resists, your legs burn, your muscles fatigue, and your biological instinct tells you to stop. However, you push past it because you know that growth, strength, and progress lie beyond initial discomfort.

The goal is to use this push beyond feedback, both physically and emotionally, to move away from zero — and thus away from being purely reactive — and progress towards ten. It is here that we can consciously choose our behavior, emotions, and mindset, rather than being controlled by them.

This is the real evolution of masculinity — to move beyond animalistic survival instincts and into a state of intentional self-mastery and true strength.

The limitations of the biological body

Our biological instincts are designed for survival, not fulfillment. Fear, stress, and desire are not inherently bad; they are natural responses deeply rooted in our evolutionary history. These instincts once served a clear purpose — to keep us alive in dangerous, unpredictable environments. The problem is that these same primal reactions often keep us trapped in cycles of reactivity and responding to modern challenges with outdated, survival-based programming.

The higher Self allows us to transcend these instincts and recognize when we act out of habit, fear, or ego rather than from a place of awareness and intention. It enables us to step back, widen our perspective, and approach life — not as a reaction to external pressures but as a conscious, chosen response. The more we cultivate this ability, the less we are ruled by biological impulses, and the more we operate from a place of clarity, self-mastery, and purpose.

The story entangled between the lines begins to emerge.

The words authenticity, spirituality, and being one's true self all mean the same thing. To be authentic, to be one's Self (with an upper case 'S'), to be spiritual, to have the power to shed Darwinian or biological urges and become something greater than our base instincts — these are all the same.

The real message hidden between the lines is that to be ourselves, we must remove the things that stop us from reaching that potential. Remember, the goal is not to mimic, adopt, follow, emulate, act like, pretend, or operate from ego. If we are not supposed to act like something we are not, then how do we be ourselves?

We stop being anything else. We stop acting like something we were conditioned to be. We stop chasing approval, stop performing, stop living based on expectations, and stop acting like animals ruled by Darwinian instincts. And when you stop being all those things that you are not, the real you will finally emerge. The you that stopped pretending to be tough, or braggy to impress someone when the word you used didn't feel right.

To put a closing cap on this transition from zero to ten, the progression from animal (zero) to spirit (ten), has also been captured by Dr. David Hawkins in his scale of consciousness. As one moves up the scale, something also happens to one's consciousness. Dr. Hawkins has used kinesiology to construct his scale of consciousness. Hawkins developed the "Map of Consciousness", a logarithmic scale ranging from 1 to 1,000, to quantify levels of human consciousness. This scale illustrates the progression from lower states, like shame and guilt, to higher states, such as love, joy, and enlightenment. According to Hawkins' research, as individuals ascend this scale, they experience increased clarity, peace, and alignment with their higher Self, akin to the quotation by Einstein stated earlier in the book.

For those interested in diving deeper into how consciousness levels can be understood, Dr. Hawkins' body of work is worth exploring.

Nietzsche explained it like this in *Thus Spoke Zarathustra*: imagine a rope stretched out over a ravine. On one end is "man as beast," on the other, "man as god." And there we are, each of us, walking across that rope. For Nietzsche, man was not a finished product but a bridge. He saw our current form as a transition between the animal on one end of the rope and on the other side the higher, self-created being.

He goes on to explain that beneath the rope lies the abyss: chaos, failure, meaninglessness. He notes that the crossing is unsafe and even precarious. Nietzsche writes that Zarathustra, the character in the book, warns a crowd about this rope, but they laugh and mock him as they shout, preferring comfort, convention, and animal instinct over transformation. All this was written in the 1880s. It reads today like a description of social media mobs and TikTok trends: the herd dictating how we should act, and ridiculing anyone who dares to evolve.

Conclusion

Nietzsche saw man as incomplete. The walk over the rope itself, the struggle to cross, is the point. Many will never step onto the rope at all. But he insisted there was something noble in the attempt, as I do. He saw it as noble even in failure, compared to those who continually choose safety over growth.

What do you think society would be like if more took his book and the walk along the rope more seriously then?

That rope is the Vector of Self Mastery I describe. On one side is the beast: fear, desire, survival. On the other hand, there is the spiritual: wisdom, compassion, freedom, and self-mastery. Every step either pulls us back into instinct or carries us forward toward purpose.

The rope dangerously sways, with confusion, fear, and frustration. It tempts us to fall, while unseen forces try to drag or pull us backwards to the beast side. Yet this is the work, choosing, again and again, to stay awake and keep moving forward. To keep crossing the rope as Nietzsche suggested humanity did in 1880.

On the far side of Nietzsche's rope lies his vision of the Übermensch—the one who creates his own values, free from herd morality, fear, and borrowed rules. In Alphas Die Early, I call this crossing the path of the Omega Man. Where Nietzsche spoke of man becoming "more than man," I see it as evolving beyond Homo sapiens as mere participants in the animal kingdom into highly conscious, spiritual beings. For Nietzsche, the Übermensch embodied self-overcoming, radical authenticity, and strength. For us, the Omega Man carries those same qualities, tempered with heart, compassion, and freedom.

Will you try to cross the rope?

Part II:

Breaking the Cycle

Chapter 4:

A New Masculinity — The Non-Masculine Male

What is non-masculinity that is ultimately masculinity in disguise?

The fact that this sentence even needs to be written in such a way speaks to the immense bastardization of the term masculinity for any reader of this book.

If someone asked you to define masculinity, what would you say?

Likely, it would be something similar to what I would have said. Yet, as this paragraph suggests and as discussed in earlier chapters, the definition of masculinity varies widely, shifting from social group to social group, peer to peer, and country to country. This alone proves how fluid and inconsistent the term has become.

Truth be told, I was just as confused by this definition of masculinity. Especially when surrounded by other men engaged in locker room talk filled with bravado, exaggeration, and posturing. They talked about things I'd never even thought of, and yet somehow, I was supposed to nod along, participate, and prove that I belonged. I remember laughing when they laughed, even when I didn't fully understand what was so funny. I remember forcing myself to appear interested, trying to mirror their confidence and fit in with the group. But deep down, I felt like I was faking it. I felt like I was failing some test I didn't even know I'd signed up for.

It made me feel not only like less of a man but, at times, like I should avoid anything that might even be perceived as unmanly, including, apparently, quiche.

This brings to mind the satirical book *Real Men Don't Eat Quiche*, published in 1982 by Bruce Fierstein, which poked fun at the shifting, often absurd expectations of masculinity at the time. The book humorously outlined men's social pressures to conform to hyper-masculine stereotypes, mocking the idea that "real men" had to act tough, avoid emotions, and reject anything remotely associated with sophistication or sensitivity — right down to their food choices. Seriously, how many times have you heard the phrase "real men eat steak"?

So many times, I tried to be the man I thought I was supposed to be: strong, unemotional, unaffected, or important. But in those moments, when I felt like an outsider in a conversation I didn't belong in, I wasn't strong at all. I was just pretending. And that pretense? It was exhausting. Needless to say, it wasn't me. It looked like me, as it was a pretense of me.

And to make matters worse, I did like steak! I also liked shrimp and rainbow sherbet. How manly did that come off?

The satire of *Real Men Don't Eat Quiche* rings just as true today. Masculinity has long been shaped by arbitrary, culturally defined rules from what men should eat to how they should talk, behave, or even think. And yet, the more we try to fit into a definition that isn't truly ours, the further we stray from being an authentic man. I spent years trying to perform masculinity, waiting for some moment when it would feel natural and when I would finally feel like I belonged. But maybe belonging wasn't the answer. Maybe the real question isn't whether I measured up but why I ever felt like I had to prove it in the first place.

If we have to prove masculinity, is it masculinity at all?

Many would say "Yes" to this question, but why?

Should something as fundamental as a definition of "masculinity " need to be proven by actions, especially when we know it's defined so differently across cultures and time periods (generational) without any clear, published standard or action for men to follow? After all, masculinity is often associated with success, yet we lack a concrete definition of what success truly means.

At present, masculinity is largely dictated by societal expectations where, according to the etymology of 'masculate', "boys and men are rewarded in a variety of settings such as schools, intimate relationships, the workplace, military, and prisons for adhering to these stereotypic expectations."

However, when we look at the evolution of the definitions of masculinity, to be masculine mostly meant to just be male.

The evolution of the definition of masculinity

From Etymonline, we can see that the definitions are largely based on masculinity being defined as 'male', with definitions being based on biology more than other factors[1]:

- 12th century, from Latin *masculinus*, "male, of masculine gender," from *masculus*, "male, masculine; worthy of a man," diminutive of *mas* (genitive maris), "male person, male,"

- mid-14th century, "belonging to the male grammatical gender."

- Late 14th century, "of men, of the male sex," from the Old French *masculin* "of the male sex," a word of unknown origin. The diminutive form might be achieved by pairing association with *femininus*. Meaning "having the appropriate qualities of the male sex, physically or mentally.

17th century

In the mid-1600s, masculinity was largely defined by traits such as being "manly, virile, and powerful." These qualities were deeply tied to physical strength, bravery, and dominance, qualities essential for survival and leadership in an agrarian and often dangerous society (Connell,1995).

References

1. Etymonline (retrieved 2025)

In the 17th century, survival depended on physical labor, hunting, and protection, emphasizing masculine traits like physical strength and endurance (Kimmel, 1996). Strictly defined gender roles often framed men as action-takers and leaders, associating masculinity with dominance and control over one's environment (Rotundo, 1993).

Masculinity has also been shaped by religious frameworks, where men were seen as heads of households with moral and spiritual authority, and responsibility for maintaining the family's virtue and safety (Carter, 1993).

Regardless of the time period, definitions of masculinity are primarily based on the biological reality of being male. A male, by anatomy, possesses greater strength and stamina (the presence of testosterone), naturally falling into roles that mirror those of other male species in the animal kingdom.

Of course, there are exceptions — the bald eagle, the humpback whale, and the black widow spider, to name a few — where the female is stronger and sometimes even dominates or overpowers the male, with the black widow often even consuming the male after mating. (Eagle Eye Adventures, 2024; Pacific Whale Foundation, 2024; National Geographic, 2024).

Post World War 2

In 1945, post-WWII, masculinity began to be characterized by social behavior. Advantages were no longer supported by male biological traits, such as strength and virility, but by behaviors like being a protector and provider. These were shaped heavily by war experiences and economic rebuilding (Coontz, 1992).

The soldier returning home as a hero became the ultimate masculine archetype, celebrated for strength, sacrifice, and stoicism — all qualities glorified in war films and media (Bourke, 1999).

The rise of the nuclear family emphasized the role of men as breadwinners, with women relegated to domestic roles. Men's self-worth became tied to their ability to provide financially (Coontz, 1992). And in films and advertisements, masculinity was portrayed as stoic and rugged, with figures like John Wayne reinforcing the ideal of emotional restraint and external success (Cohan, 1997).

This shift from agrarian to industrial jobs linked masculinity to productivity and hard work. As such, success was measured by career advancement, income, and material possessions (Kimmel, 1996). This is also the birth of the masculinity archetype.

The 1950s–60s

Men were expected to conform to strict roles as breadwinners and stoic leaders. Any deviation from these norms was stigmatized, creating a narrow definition of masculinity (Rotundo 1993).

The Cold War heightened the ideal of masculinity as strong, patriotic, and ready to defend democracy against communism. Strength and control became national imperatives for men (Dudziak, 2000).

While the 1960s counterculture challenged many traditional roles, masculinity remained relatively untouched in mainstream culture (Connell, 1995).

The 1970s-80s

Feminism and women's rights rose, and traditional gender roles started to be questioned. In addition, masculinity faced increasing scrutiny as a social construct. Many men, however, doubled down on traditional roles to reaffirm their identity (Faludi, 1999).

As more women entered the workforce, the traditional male role as sole provider began to erode, causing anxiety about what it meant to "be a man" (Coontz, 2011).

Figures like Bruce Springsteen emerged as more complex masculine role models, balancing traditional ruggedness with introspection, although the "rugged individual" ideal remained dominant (Cohan 1997).

The 1990s-2000s

Discussions about mental health and gender equality brought masculinity into a more introspective phase, challenging traditional norms (Kimmel, 2000).

Some men felt threatened by women's progress, leading to the emergence of "men's rights" movements and a resurgence of hyper-masculine ideals (Faludi, 1999).

A more fashion-conscious, emotionally expressive version of masculinity (dubbed "metrosexual") gained popularity but faced backlash for being "too feminine" (Simpson, 1996).

2010s to Present

The term "toxic masculinity" became widely recognized, describing harmful behaviors and attitudes arising from suppressing vulnerability and emphasizing dominance and aggression (Connell, 1995).

Concepts like emotional intelligence, vulnerability, and authenticity are increasingly celebrated as masculine virtues. However, toxic social media figures who continue to fight against those traits and promote hyper-masculine, alpha ideals have begun to redefine the archetype once again (Kimmel, 2013).

Social media platforms amplify unrealistic standards (e.g., fitness influencers) and challenge traditional ideals by promoting diverse representations of men (Twenge, 2017).

Figures like Barack Obama and Keanu Reeves began to serve as modern examples of masculinity that balance strength with empathy, humility, and authenticity (Connell, 2000). However, these traits remain constantly under attack with a push to redefine the definition.

At Benedictine College in May 2024, Harrison Butker, the Kansas City Chiefs kicker, made remarks widely criticized as misogynistic, homophobic, and racist. He suggested that women should prioritize homemaking over careers. His speech ignited widespread backlash, sparking debate about the intersection of personal beliefs and public influence. (*The Nation, May 2024; The Guardian, August 2024; The Sun, May 2024.*)

This shift has also encouraged men to reject and even attack anything that opposes the current definition of masculinity, including anything considered stereotypically feminine, suppressing emotions (except anger), and distancing themselves both emotionally and physically from other men. It has prioritized competition, success, and power while reinforcing anti-femininity and homophobia. These are not inherent male traits but learned behaviors that are shaped by shifting social norms. To show the contradiction and absurdity, why would one be considered a real man or masculine, with the self-depiction of confidence and bravado, need to fight off anything as a threat, let alone femininity?

Are masculine men afraid of losing their masculinity? Is that confidence and strength?

In the past seventy-five years, the definition of masculinity has evolved more rapidly than in the previous seven centuries.

We have moved from a biological definition to one now rooted in behavioral norms. These norms vary from region to region, and decade to decade, and shift according to societal changes. Can you see why there's a masculinity crisis? The definition is constantly being rewritten to reflect whatever happens to be culturally popular at the time, leaving men with no stable foundation to follow.

What's most interesting to me is that Barack Obama and Keanu Reeves became popular for reasons entirely unrelated to masculinity. Yet, their success led young men to model their behavioral traits as a new form of masculinity.

Young men see John Wick, a badass character, and the overwhelming popularity of Keanu Reeves, and they internalize his demeanor as a blueprint for success. But is this true masculinity or merely the byproduct of marketing, timing, and cultural trends? Was Reeves' appeal a result of his personal character, or was it a combination of screenwriting, special effects, and Hollywood's ability to manufacture an idealized figure?

Regardless, success itself became the model. Young men observed Reeves' public image and began emulating his traits, believing that adopting his calm, mysterious, humble persona might yield them similar respect and admiration.

For women, a parallel can be drawn to the Jennifer Aniston haircut, famously known as "The Rachel". This hairstyle debuted in 1995 during the first season of Friends and quickly became a cultural phenomenon. Hair salons worldwide reported overwhelming demand, with some stylists stating that the Rachel accounted for nearly 40% of their business at its peak. However, its widespread appeal wasn't just about the hairstyle itself; it was largely driven by Aniston's rising celebrity status, proving how success and popularity shape trends not just in behavior but also in appearance. (Wikipedia)

However, a biological difference exists in how men and women process success and desirability. Women's evolutionary instincts tend to align with beauty and attractiveness, responding to visual cues of desirability. Meanwhile, men's Darwinian instincts prompt them to mimic behavior, associating success with actions rather than aesthetics.

Make no mistake, for both men and women, success isn't purely about looks but about behavior. Young men copy the mannerisms of successful men, whether or not those traits are authentic or universally effective. There is even a name for this transitory definition of manhood from anatomy to behavior — hegemonic masculinity.

"In contemporary American and European culture, [hegemonic masculinity] serves as the standard upon which the "real man" is defined. According to [R. W.] Connell, contemporary hegemonic masculinity is built on two legs: domination of women and a hierarchy of intermale dominance. Today's hegemonic masculinity in the United States of America and Europe includes a high degree of ruthless competition, an inability to express emotions other than anger, an unwillingness to admit weakness or dependency, devaluation of women and all feminine attributes in men, homophobia, and so forth." (Kupers:2005).

At its core, this is Darwinian survival instinct at play. Men observe the most "successful" male at a given time and instinctively attempt to mirror his behaviors, hoping it will grant them higher status, more power, or increased desirability.

The same pattern applies to the 2025 election. Trump's success, whether defined by his push to eliminate wasteful government spending or his efforts to reduce the U.S. national debt, has made him a figure for young men to observe and emulate. His traits and behaviors have become a model for what some believe men should embody today. However, just as it is misguided to mimic Keanu Reeves' persona as a blueprint for masculinity, it is equally a mistake to imitate Trump's traits as a definitive guide for how men should behave.

To mimic others is to lose our true selves.

When something new becomes popular, do we simply change and adopt those traits? No. The only clear path to being a man is to be yourself.

This doesn't mean you can't be a fan of Keanu Reeves or Donald Trump. Admire whoever you want, but don't mistake admiration for imitation. Behave like you. Shed anything that isn't truly yours.

Einstein once wrote: *"A man should look for what is and not for what he thinks should be."* To me, that reminder is rooted in clarity, not conformity, and can rescue us from the drive for performance and the trap underlying it. For further weight, I feel Einstein's work was grounded in measurable truths, making him an ideal figure to illustrate the importance of authenticity over imitation.

As the beginning of Part II of this book, "Breaking the Cycle," in this chapter, I propose that to redefine masculinity, we must shed the performative behaviors dictated by undefined, trial-and-error societal norms and embrace a solid, authentic definition instead. As discussed in earlier chapters, we must change our approach. Defining masculinity merely as a gender, as done in the 1200s to the 1700s, is insufficient in today's hyper-connected, idol-centric society. Additionally, defining masculinity as behaviors matching perceptions of successful men, as done from WWII until the present day, is equally insufficient.

The new definition of masculinity should focus on strength, success, and sustainability. Through my experiences, I've realized that the greatest strength lies in being true to oneself. It requires courage to discern genuine strength from the mere appearance of strength. Expressing vulnerability and authenticity in the face of perceived strength is true power.

Consider the story of the Buddha and the angry elephant. Devadatta, driven by jealousy, sought to harm the Buddha by releasing a furious elephant named Nalagiri into his path. Nalagiri, drunk and enraged, charged through the streets, trampling everything in its way. Townspeople fled in terror as the beast barreled toward the Buddha. Instead of reacting with fear or attempting to run, the Buddha remained perfectly still, his presence unwavering.

As the elephant neared, the Buddha extended his hand and softly spoke to Nalagiri, radiating pure compassion and loving kindness. The elephant, overwhelmed by this powerful energy, began to slow its charge. Despite its violent conditioning, it was unable to continue its rampage in the presence of such serenity. The Buddha's deep inner peace transformed the beast's fury into submission, and Nalagiri, once uncontrollable, stopped in front of him, bowing its massive head in reverence. The Buddha then gently touched Nalagiri's head, calming it further, demonstrating that true strength lies not in physical dominance or aggression but in the ability to remain centered, in control of oneself, and to influence others through unwavering inner power.

Similarly, the iconic image from the Tiananmen Square protests in 1989, known as "Tank Man," captures the essence of quiet strength. An unidentified man, carrying only two shopping bags, stood alone before a column of advancing tanks. Despite the overwhelming force in front of him, he refused to move. His unarmed, fearless defiance halted the tanks, if only for a moment, yet that moment became a global symbol of resistance against oppression. He had no weapons, no army behind him, just the sheer will to stand for what he believed in. This moment exemplifies how true strength often manifests through vulnerability and steadfastness in the face of overwhelming force.

These examples underscore that redefining masculinity involves embracing authenticity, courage, and compassion, rather than conforming to societal expectations or performative behaviors.

I bet the phrase "be yourself" raises several questions. It certainly did for me. That's why we will explore what it means to embody this form of masculinity and how to achieve it, how to live authentically, and how to be fully yourself.

The key is to stop trying to be a perception. Break the cycle of the clichéd definitions of masculinity that have shifted with every era. Stop performing. Let go of the charade and embrace who you truly are. I understand, as I, too, wore armor of misdirection. I pretended to be something that I am not for personal gain. I now know my motivation was to "survive" or to do better, or to be seen as better, and to have tried to do more for status. I remember times in my life when I was overly competitive. I'd call out other men's flaws, not because they were truly flaws, but so I could make myself look better than them.

Now, however, I can recall moments of success and just smile silently and spiritually to myself, without any need for validation or competition.

Chapter 4: A new masculinity wrap

This chapter invites you to reflect on what it truly means to be a non-masculine/masculine man and an authentic man.

The goal is to listen to the quiet voice that encourages growth, authenticity, and connection. A voice that remains present even when drowned out by the loud, booming sound of Darwinian urges pushing you to be "The Fittest." This voice is your internal compass, guiding you toward your highest potential. Accessing your higher self requires quieting the noise of the external world and tuning into your inner wisdom.

It's a journey that involves integrating spirituality, self-awareness, and intentional practices into your daily life. It's about learning to be fully yourself rather than conforming to external expectations. It's about recognizing that you can transcend the limitations of fear and ego, and align with your truest potential.

This path is not always easy. It demands shedding old conditioning, rejecting the pressure to perform, and embracing an identity that is truly your own. But while the journey may be challenging, the rewards for peace, purpose, and genuine fulfillment are immeasurable.

Next Chapter

In Chapter 5, we will continue to dive into the brutally honest realities needed to break the cycle. This cycle doesn't just exist within us; it extends into every aspect of our lives, shaping our relationships, our interactions, and the way we move through the world.

The people closest to us, our inner circles, can provide some of the greatest lessons and the strongest support for real change. Recognizing these influences, understanding their impact, and reshaping them with intention is a crucial part of the journey.

The road to truth is not loud, but steady. Stay the course. Your real self is worth it.

Comments From Brad Kearns

Dave has introduced me to interesting concepts like the David Hawkins scale, and this chapter provided a great overview of the general idea of evolving to a higher level than animals and pursuing self-mastery. I'm always inspired when talking to Dave about these concepts, or when reading books or listening to podcasts on this subject matter.

One thing I notice that happens to me regularly: my best intentions and awareness of self-mastery skills desert me when I need them the most! Very frustrating. From my study and deep interest in the subject, I know the best way to respond when conversations gets heated; I know the actions and thoughts I should execute to pull me out of a rut; I know about a big picture perspective that I can shift to in a moment to help me escape from whining, complaining, feeling like a victim, or losing control. And I'm great at giving advice to others when they're struggling (aren't we all?) But...where do my skills go when I'm under pressure?

When things calm down, I'm great with post-mortem analysis, processing the lessons learned, becoming a better person through experience, and so forth. Then, when the next crisis of the mind or situation comes along, there I go again - reverting to fear response or whatever.

Lately, I've been doing a good job of giving myself permission to be imperfect without judgement or negativity. I think judging oneself harshly is part of the rut, you know what I mean? For example, when you feel guilty about something, it's a way of giving yourself permission to repeat the behavior or remain stuck. For example, you've been so busy lately that you haven't called or written grandma. You know how she loves hearing from you, it makes her day! But hey, all that business travel and overflowing inbox, there's no time for everything.

Because you feel guilty, it makes you a good person who loves your grandma and has just been super busy. If you didn't feel guilty, you'd be a selfish, uncaring asshole who can't even lift a finger for an old lady who shuffles to her mail slot every day at the nursing home, hoping there might be a letter from you. That's the game we play with ourselves. Similarly, be wary of that tendency to offer a reflexive apology every time you misbehave or let others down. Instead, try to live your life in such a way that you don't have to apologize for your behavior, nor feel guilty. Granted, heartfelt apologies are certainly appropriate in many occasions, just don't hide behind them, nor behind guilt. Go for it! Cross the rope!

Chapter 5:

Recognizing the Scripts to Break — Relationships & Childhood Programming

Like it or not, life is shaped by relationships. They influence our happiness, even though they were never meant to be our sole source of it. True happiness must come from within, from a sustainable inner foundation, not from the shifting weather of other people's moods or approval. Relationships, however, can bring us joy, frustration, or heartbreak. They shouldn't hold that power, but they often do.

You don't need a romantic partner to feel the impact of a "significant other." A boss, sibling, business partner, or friend can occupy just as central a role in your emotional world. Relationships come in many forms, and all of them, whether we are aware of it or not, can shape our journey.

Relationships are one of the most powerful tools for self-discovery. Carl Jung famously said, "Everything that irritates us about others can lead us to an understanding of ourselves." This profound insight captures the essence of relationships as mirrors that reflect our internal world. They show us where we still need to grow — but only if we're willing to pay attention.

In this chapter, we'll expose the personas we wear in relationships, understand why we created them in the first place, and then look at how we can replace them with the kind of truth that can sustain love, connection, and self-respect.

The trap of false personas in relationships

How often do we blame others for how we feel without realizing we're reacting to a version of ourselves we created just to be liked? How often do we act unauthentically in relationships, changing our behavior to gain approval, avoid abandonment, or control how others see us? If we're constantly mirroring societal figures or the trending "Alpha Male" of the moment — be it Keanu Reeves' quiet mystery or Trump's brash dominance — how sustainable is that approach?

What happens when the world changes its mind about what earns respect? Do we shapeshift again? And again?

When we engage in relationships, not as ourselves but as the version we believe will win affection, we are connecting two "false selves." This dynamic often creates fragile, unstable relationships. Why? Because the foundation is fake. It's a performance, not a bond or a transaction, and not an authentic convergence of people.

Authentic relationships are not about pretending to be something we're not. They thrive on consistency, being genuine, and showing up as who we are. Relationships should be an extension of our authenticity, not a chosen mask meant for success or a staged performance to appease an audience, even if that audience is just one person. If you constantly mold yourself to align with someone else's expectations, what happens when those expectations change? What happens when they stop being impressed by the mask? Can a relationship built on adaptation ever be solid?

Eckhart Tolle writes that when we're not being ourselves, we act based on who we think we are, and treat others based on who we think they are. More importantly, we treat them based on who we think they are in relation to who we think we are. Essentially, we're judging a false version of ourselves against a false version of them.

Even funnier is that they're doing the same thing. Two people. Four masks.

This drive to portray a false persona intensifies when the relationship feels like a lifeline for our unfulfilled goals or personal needs, and when we look to someone else to fix what only we can heal. The survival mechanism kicks in and does things to modify, mimic, or exude a false self to stay safe.

Yet, we still expect a deep, meaningful connection. And then we wonder why that connection feels hollow, shaky, or fake — even though it was built on a foundation of pretense.

Can you see the need to be truly yourself in relationships?

Survival vs. authenticity: The peer pressure loop

Have you ever said yes when you meant no, just to be accepted? Perhaps you drank something you didn't want to? Pretended to like something just to fit in? Acted a certain way to impress someone, even though it wasn't really you?

These moments aren't just social awkwardness — they're signs. They're reflections of our survival instincts at play. They reveal that, deep down, our survival instincts are still in control. This is what I call a "learned relationship." We learn how to behave in a group — not for connection but to earn validation. It's just another form of Darwinian survival.

Research confirms it: seeking external validation erodes authenticity.

Performance-driven self-worth can turn individuals into "emotionless learning machines," disconnecting them from who they truly are[1] (Psychology Today). In addition, chasing approval distorts self-perception, making it increasingly difficult to live authentically (Psych Central).

Darwin's "survival of the fittest" theory doesn't just apply to the jungle; it governs the schoolyard, the boardroom, and the dating app. We act to conform. We act to fit in. We act to survive the moment. But what happens when we shape-shift our persona to fit what's currently admired, only to find the social landscape has shifted again?

References

1. Psychology Today

Do we modify it once more? Do we perform again? Change again? Shrink again?

The cycle continues. This is why "knowing better" isn't enough. You can't think your way out of instincts. You have to rewire them. The goal is to beat it.

Let's face it: something in our lives will eventually stop working, forcing us to re-evaluate. However, if our friendships, relationships, and careers are built on a version of ourselves that isn't real, what might happen when we stop pretending? Do they all collapse when we show up as our authentic selves?

Often, yes.

Relationships built on performance fade when the act ends. But what about the ones that survive authenticity? Simply, those are the ones that last.

The Buddha once said, "The moment you stop chasing validation is the moment you find peace."

The unsustainability of relationship façades: A lesson from Crimson Tide

Take the movie *Crimson Tide* as a perfect metaphor. At a critical moment, Lieutenant Weps, played by Viggo Mortensen, is caught in a mutiny aboard a nuclear submarine. He initially sides with Denzel Washington's character, the executive officer. The film frames his decision as a moral one, but beneath the surface, it's mostly a survival analysis determining Wep's decision.

Later, Weps switches his allegiance to Gene Hackman's character, the captain. Why? Because it looked like the captain was regaining control. Siding with him now offered a better chance of survival.

What was Weps' reasoning?

The other officers say, "Think of your family" — a reminder that choosing against the captain could come at a personal cost.

Weps replies, "I'm thinking about my family."

It wasn't a stand for truth. It was a calculation. A move made not from values, but from fear.

This moment illustrates one of the most dangerous traps in relationships — choosing self-preservation over authenticity. The instinct to survive can easily override morals and values.

Biologically, survival has always been our first instinct.

Here's the thing — we are no longer just animals. We've evolved past the caveman reflex — but we're still carrying a two-million-year-old survival program alongside just 45,000 years of conscious thinking.

Old software. New hardware. Conflict guaranteed.

Often, we rationalize self-preserving decisions to protect our ego, even when we know deep down they violate our integrity. Have you ever made a choice that felt wrong but seemed necessary at the time? A choice you justified to yourself, even as your body told you it was off? Like Weps, we shift our stances, behaviors, and loyalties based on perceived safety.

Self-preserving choices create fragile relationships that are built on shifting sand. Eventually, you're faced with a choice: do I show up for real, or keep playing the role that gets applause? That choice doesn't just define your relationships, it also shapes them. It defines your life. It's the classic post-rationalization: "It felt like a good idea at the time."

What happens when we see someone stand for truth at their own cost?

We revere it. Think of Tank Man in Tiananmen Square. He stood still and changed the world. As bystanders, we admire that courage. We say: "I don't know if I could have done that." We feel awe because we know, on some level, what it takes to break free from survival and act from the soul.

Authenticity is not convenient, but it is durable. It fosters the kind of relationships that don't require manipulation, adaptation, or performance to thrive. They survive because they're real.

The path forward: Choosing authenticity over adaptation

So ask yourself: are you living in accordance with your values or reacting to someone else's expectations? Are your relationships rooted in who you really are, or who you perform to be? What if you dropped the performance? What would happen if you just showed up as you?

These aren't easy questions—but they're necessary ones.

True strength in relationships comes from resisting these pressures and choosing conscious, values-based action. The goal isn't to mold yourself into what society deems "successful" this week. The goal is to build relationships that support the person you are, not the persona you've worn to be liked.

As noted, key relationships are essential. But should you be staying in a relationship by slightly altering who you are? That slow erosion doesn't serve anyone — not you and not them.

Where it all begins: Childhood programming

If relationships are one of the most significant forces shaping our lives, then our first relationships with our parents, siblings, and caretakers are where it all begins. These early dynamics become the blueprint for our survival programming.

As infants, we don't just learn behavior. We absorb the rules of love, of worth, and of belonging. We learn from how affection was given or withheld, how conflict was handled, and whether truth was welcomed or punished.

These unspoken patterns become the template we carry into adulthood.

If our first relationships required adaptation for acceptance, or if our childhood environment was unpredictable, chaotic, or emotionally unavailable, then our subconscious absorbed those lessons as survival tactics. Unless we reprogram those early survival codes, we'll keep living from them long after they stop serving us.

Childhood programming

What air is to the lungs — an unstoppable flow of oxygen keeping us alive — is what blood is to the heart, and is what thinking is to the brain. The brain drives our survival instincts. It is unconscious, myopic, automatic, and relentless. No matter how much wisdom we accumulate, our bodies and behaviors are wired for one thing above all — to stay alive.

What does it actually mean to "save your life"? In modern times, the answer varies wildly. Cultural background, geography, class, and social norms all shape what "survival" looks like for each individual. This includes how we were raised, how many siblings we had, our birth order, how our parents treated each other, and the overall emotional tone of our early home. That early survival definition is embedded deep within our subconscious. And, unless examined, it quietly but powerfully runs the show for decades.

The burrow: How childhood survival shapes adult reality

Imagine a baby bunny — let's call him Bugs — is born into a burrow. Everything Bugs knows is shaped by this tiny underground world: his siblings, the food available, the protective presence (or absence) of his father, and the warmth of his mother.

To Bugs, this burrow isn't just home — it's the entire universe. If something disrupts that world — if a predator invades, or the burrow collapses, or a flood comes — Bugs is suddenly unprepared. His chance of survival plummets. Why? Because the burrow he knows and was built to survive in — his world — no longer exists.

Humans are no different. As infants, our "burrow" includes our home, our caregivers, and our environment. It's where we learn language and habits, and also who we need to be to feel safe, loved, and accepted. Even birth order can shape the programming. Firstborns, for example, experience a world without siblings — until they don't. Second children are born into a dynamic that is already in motion. Every change in that dynamic alters the environment to which each child adapts.

Unlike animals, however, humans don't stay in one burrow. We move a lot. And even if we don't physically move, our environment constantly shifts. Parents change or get divorced. Culture evolves. Norms change.

With each shift, our internal survival strategies get tested. Humans are still bound by the genetic principle of adapting to our environment. The difference is that our environments now change faster than our biology. That's why re-adaptation and conscious reprogramming is no longer optional. It's Survival 2.0.

Reprogramming through movement: Why childhood instability sticks

Do you want proof that childhood programming sticks? Consider the study on the effects on children when their family moves a lot — not emotionally, but geographically.

Each relocation forces a child to re-learn the rules of survival: new schools, new social dynamics, new cues for what's "normal." A child who moves frequently isn't just adjusting; they're recalibrating their identity each time.

Studies show that children who move often face disadvantages across multiple areas of their life, not because moving is inherently bad, but because the brain craves a stable blueprint for survival.

Here's the bottom line: your childhood programmed you. You didn't choose the environment. You didn't have a filter for what entered your psyche. There was no spam folder. No firewall. You didn't even know it was happening. Maybe until now.

Yet, it's during this exact window when we are most unaware that many of our lifelong habits and emotional defaults are hard-coded. It's like being handed a pair of glasses you didn't choose and not realizing they're tinted. Everything you see is now filtered through that lens.

If your father was loud and angry, you may have learned to yell to survive. Or you may have learned to stay silent. Either way, your response wasn't "you." It was your programming.

For me, it was growing up in a household with an attorney father. Mine was a burrow that contained arguing, fighting to be right, and presenting reasons or 'evidence' to win the argument.

The research: How moving (geographically) affects a child's future

The following research isn't here to depress you; it's here to validate what your nervous system already knows— frequent change in childhood leaves a mark. Below are just a few of the many ways that residential instability can shape a child's life outcomes.

- *Academic performance*

Research shows that frequent childhood moves are linked to lower academic performance. Residential mobility disrupts school connectedness, diminishes a child's sense of belonging, and undermines academic self-esteem. These factors raise the risk of long-term academic struggle. (Langenkamp, 2019)

- *Economic mobility*

Children who move frequently are less likely to achieve upward economic mobility as adults. Instability during the formative years can reduce educational achievement and hinder future career growth. (Chetty et.al., 2014)

- *Relationship dissolution*

Adults who experienced three or more moves in childhood, before the age of 17, have a 55% higher likelihood of divorce or unstable romantic relationships. Why? Frequent childhood relocations may disrupt the ability to form and maintain deep, lasting connections. (Salmela-Aro et al, 2019)

- *Life satisfaction*

Adolescents who move frequently report lower overall life satisfaction as adults. Disrupted friendships, weakened support systems, and fragmented social identity lead to long-term emotional effects. (Schnettle et al., 2024)

These aren't just numbers. They're proof that your nervous system isn't overreacting; it's remembering.

The burrow: The survival instinct that no longer serves us

Our survival programming is deeply tied to stability, but when that stability is constantly disrupted, the results are anything but stable.

That's why the theme of this chapter, 'recognizing the scripts to break', is so important.

If we don't take control of our reprogramming, we'll continue executing old scripts. Many of these scripts are written in fear, in chaos, and in circumstances that don't exist anymore.

It's critical to understand how we're wired, both through millions of years of DNA and the first five years of our lives. Those wires still drive our choices, especially in relationships. Until we see them clearly, we'll keep repeating the cycle — shape-shifting, people-pleasing, self-erasing.

Today's world is nothing like the one in which our ancestors evolved. However, our instincts don't know that, so we're still running two-million-year-old programming in a world that now demands emotional intelligence, adaptability, and self-awareness.

The challenge is to evolve without losing ourselves. For those of us who moved around a lot as children, that challenge is doubled. Every move required that we redefine the burrow, learn new rules, and build new strategies — often with zero guidance. Research confirms that frequent childhood moves destabilize identity, limit long-term success, and hinder relational depth.

But the bigger issue isn't the move; it's the absence of reprogramming after the move.

We grow up, but we don't stop updating the operating system.

Let's suppose we don't look back at what we absorbed as kids. If we don't consciously upgrade the outdated software we inherited, we end up living trapped by instincts that don't fit reality, and we won't even know we're doing it.

The survival paradox and the Dunning-Kruger effect

Here's the paradox of old survival programming — it doesn't just keep us reactive, it makes us dangerously overconfident, often by misunderstanding rather than real innate confidence. This is where the Dunning-Kruger effect comes in.

The Dunning-Kruger effect encompasses the psychological principle that those with the least competence tend to overestimate their abilities the most. When we operate on assumptions instead of awareness, we misread the room and ourselves. We think we've got it handled, but we don't. We end up living in a perception of reality, not reality itself. Our burrow-defined lens gives us a false sense of confidence. We think we know "how the world works" when we've only ever seen our tiny piece of it.

It's not true; it's just programming. And when we finally step outside that illusion, when the real world doesn't match our script, we are crushed.

The ram: A metaphor for misguided confidence

Picture two rams, horns locked, charging at each other with blind determination. A ram doesn't strategize. It doesn't calculate the odds. It only knows what it's been wired to do.

So it charges forward. Sometimes, it loses. Yet, even after being knocked unconscious, the ram wakes up and does it again. Why? Because instinct is all it knows.

This is precisely what happens when we let our old programming run the show. Convinced we're right, we charge into jobs, relationships, and arguments. Too late, we find out that we're outmatched. Unprepared. Misguided. We weren't responding to reality; we were responding to a survival script from childhood.

Sheriff Will vs. Rambo: The consequence of overestimating yourself

One of the clearest examples of outdated confidence comes from *Rambo: First Blood*.

Sheriff Will Teasle, played by Brian Dennehy, is a small-town lawman; he's confident, dominant, and running on old programming. He sees Rambo, a quiet stranger, and assumes he can dominate him, because that's what his world has always rewarded.

But Will is playing checkers, and Rambo is playing chess. At every turn, Will loses — first in the police station, then in the wilderness, then in the helicopter pursuit, and finally in the all-out confrontation.

At no point does Will stop and ask, "Why am I losing?" Instead of reassessing, he keeps pushing forward, blindly following his instincts. He doubles down. He pushes harder. He lets the script run. At one point, Rambo's commanding officer tells Will, "You couldn't handle him in the police station. What makes you think you can now?" But Will doesn't hear it. He's charging ahead again — just like the ram.

This is what happens when we trust our ego over our awareness. We mimic the "real man" persona we were taught to play. Thinking force equals success; we push harder, and we get outplayed, outpaced, and emotionally wrecked.

We don't stop to ask what game we're playing. We lose in games we should never have entered. We overestimate because we've zoomed in too far. And it's all because we're performing, not perceiving.

Have you ever been Sheriff Will?

We've all had a Sheriff Will moment where we doubled down instead of waking up.

Convinced that grit alone will be enough, we've all tried to win against someone more skilled, more experienced, or more prepared. Maybe it was a game of pool; the other guy let us win early to bait us into a hustle. Perhaps it was in a business negotiation; we walked in confident, only to realize too late that we were outmatched and outmaneuvered.

We thought we had it handled. It wasn't actual or real confidence, though; it was instinct, yet untested, unexamined instinct.

The problem is that we aren't assessing the situation logically; we're operating off an internal script, a set of survival responses based on past experiences (i.e., programming). These experiences don't necessarily apply to the current moment either. They're all about old programming, old habits, and old reflexes in a new world. We're relying on instincts from a burrow we no longer live in.

What about the Dunning-Kruger effect?

It thrives in this environment where men think they know more than they do because their frame of reference is too small to understand what they're missing. It's the same tactic used by pool hall hustlers when they bait men who think they're better than they are.

Ego: The last animal instinct

What keeps us pushing when we should pause, reflect, or walk away?

It's this very dynamic we've been talking about throughout this entire chapter. Another word for it is ego.

The ego is a leftover survival instinct; a biological tool that enables individuals to assert dominance, defend their territory, and climb the social hierarchy.

In the wild, ego helped us mate, protect food, and lead packs. In today's world, however, ego often leads us straight into disaster. Today, where success is based on adaptability and emotional intelligence, rather than brute force, ego no longer protects us. It blinds us. It breaks us. And we don't even know it.

Sheriff Will's ego got the better of him again and again. Ours will, too, if we continue to let it drive our actions.

Performance, approval, and the cost of becoming someone else

For me, the mask looked like this: perform, appease, and cooperate all in the name of being accepted, and even loved. I learned early that people responded best when I was who they wanted me to be.

I guessed what they needed and I then became it. I put the mask on. I became what I felt was needed. Yet, it was not me. Doing this was the root of my failed marriage. To keep my partner happy, I shaped myself into the man I thought she wanted. For me, it looked like co-dependency. For her, perhaps narcissism. A common pairing: one who needs someone to bend to their will, and one who is already willing to do so.

That kind of relationship isn't built on love or growth. It's built on the need for performance and external validation. It's a desperate attempt to feel "enough."

Self-denial dehydrated me for years. It felt like walking a thousand miles through the desert, hoping for someone to say: "This matters." I intended to feel loved, and in putting in the effort to do so, I became someone other than myself.

Oprah Winfrey once said, "I became someone else just to be loved. And then I became no one." I know what that feels like. Love built on performance is not love; it's theater. And when the theater doesn't last, the result is spectacular failure.

Seeking love in the way I did was like trying to solve my dehydration problem by drinking salt water — it only made me more parched.

Breaking free from the burrow

We're wired for survival, but the wiring is old. We crave safety, but the ground keeps moving, which prevents true safety. And we overestimate ourselves because our frame of reference is still shaped by a childhood burrow we've long outgrown.

So, how do we break free? How do we rewrite the code?

Comments From Brad Kearns

Love this - hilarious! The Dunning-Kruger effect is those with the least competence tend to overestimate their abilities the most. How many times do we see extreme examples of that in daily life? The blowhards and mansplainers - aren't they so annoying and offensive?

If you answered yes, I just tricked you! Taking offense implies that you might fully recognize the role of your own ego in the story. Otherwise, why be offended? There is so much research and commentary about how flawed childhood programming plays out for the rest of our lives; it's important to be compassionate for the obstacles people have overcome to get where they are today. Everyone is doing the best they can in life with the tools they've been given. The next time you're triggered by a big egos, try pausing for a beat, smiling, and harnessing some of the skills you are learning in this book to adopt a fresh perspective.

I had some great learning in this area many years ago from my lifelong friend and former endurance running teammate, Dr. Stevey. In the running scene, people routinely fudge their reported weekly training mileage, embellish race results, and one-up other athletes during routine conversation. It's no wonder, because anyone with a grueling training regimen has to be pretty driven, pretty bad-ass, and pretty obsessed with results and social standing. You don't run 50+ miles per week and slam out painful intervals for the fun of it. Yes, there is some internal gratification involved, but it's also often about beating others and achieving social recognition.

Back in the day, I noticed a few times that when someone offered up an inflated estimation of their own abilities to Dr. Stevey (e.g., "I could probably run a 2:30 marathon with a few more months of consistent training"), he would lean into it instead of get triggered: "Oh, you can definitely break 2:30 in the marathon; I wonder about even 2:25 on a perfect day!" I'm not suggesting that you tease people with disingenuous commentary, but leaning into potentially triggering situations can feel good, and make others feel more valued too.

Chapter 5: Relationships and childhood programming wrap

In this chapter, we explored how our earliest attachments shape our definition of love, safety, and self-worth. From the moment we're born, we're taught, often unconsciously, what earns approval and what doesn't. That early programming becomes the lens through which we form every future relationship.

We've seen how unstable environments, shifting expectations, and unspoken family dynamics condition us to act inauthentically, not because we want to, but because we're wired to survive.

Left unexamined, these survival strategies don't just limit us, they distort us. They fuel overconfidence, self-erasure, and blind spots we don't even know we have.

So the real questions are:

- How do we take off a mask we didn't know we were wearing?
- How do we stop performing a role we didn't choose?
- How do we return to the person that was there before the shaping began?

Next chapter

In Chapter 6, we begin reprogramming, essentially by unprogramming, because here's the truth: long before you started performing, you were always worthy.

It's time to replace those old scripts with new ones. We want conscious scripts, not ones written by fear. We don't want scripts inherited from the burrow or based on survival. We want scripts based on choice. On truth. On who you actually are.

We'll build a new framework for living not to earn approval, but to live aligned. Not to survive the world, but to move through it as your whole, unedited self.

Are our choices rooted in our deepest values or someone else's expectations? This is what we'll explore next.

Chapter 6:

Redefining Success

For generations, "success" has been defined by external markers: wealth, power, dominance, and applause. In masculine terms, it was simple:

> *Win, and you're worthy. Lose, and you're nothing.*

If we translate animal behavior into human society, success becomes the human version of survival. But this equation, "Success = Happiness," has not only failed us but created false directional hope.

Yet, while these metrics may offer validation to the ego, they often leave the intrinsic aspects of us malnourished. That's why so many men "succeed" and still feel empty. Traditional masculinity equates a man's worth with achievement, but this narrow, shifting definition fails to capture the more profound truth of fulfillment. There's always someone richer, stronger, funnier, or more admired. The finish line keeps moving – and so does the goalpost of what it means to be "man enough."

There is always someone richer, more handsome, more creative, funnier, or, as Darwin might say, more "fit". This constant comparison not only drives us to measure our achievements against others but also leaves many men questioning whether they are manly enough. No matter how hard they try, the ideal remains ever elusive. As Theodore Roosevelt said, "Comparison is the thief of joy."

So here's the truth in practice:

> *Being the bigger peacock doesn't matter anymore.*

If your identity is built only on what others admire, then the people drawn to you won't see the real you. They'll see the feathers, not the bird.

Today's world doesn't need a louder man; it requires a deeper one. A man rooted in purpose, not posturing. In authenticity, not aggression.

The Evolutionary Trap — Why We're Wired to Compete

Our minds are still wired like hunter-gatherers. What once helped us survive now sabotages us. We're wired to scan for threats, compare ourselves to the tribe, and fight for dominance. Why does it unfold when we're sitting in traffic or scrolling Instagram?

Our evolutionary instincts, once essential for survival, now drive us into relentless competition – an outdated impulse that clashes with the complexities of modern life. As noted in contemporary reviews of the decision-making literature, evolution has endowed us with mental models and biases that are increasingly mismatched to today's complex environment.

The drive to "outdo" everyone else isn't a strength; it's a software glitch. It locks us in cycles of validation-chasing and burnout, where no win is ever enough. We're left feeling isolated, and, despite our efforts, unfulfilled. But here's the turning point: we're not merely animals driven solely by survival instincts; we have the capacity to transcend these limitations.

We must move beyond relentless instinctual drivers and programmable limitations, competition, inappropriate displays of strength, and dominance. Instead, we must focus on what truly makes us human: authenticity, connection, love, and a sense of purpose.

Warren Buffett once said that success should be measured by how many people you love and who love you back. For him, money was just a byproduct. In interviews with CNBC and Forbes, he emphasized that wealth meant little if it didn't bring peace, freedom, or meaningful relationships. This perspective resonates with the famous words of Albert Schweitzer: "Success is not the key to Happiness. Happiness is the key to success. If you love what you are doing, you will be successful."

Together, these ideas challenge the whole evolutionary script. We were taught to strut like peacocks – to display, dominate, and win. But what about fulfillment? It doesn't come from feathers, does it? As shown in today's modern world, being the biggest or flashiest should no longer be our benchmark.

Chasing external success by striving to be the "bigger peacock" creates significant mental distractions – diverting focus and attention from logic and reason – and often comes at a high cost. Men who prioritize status and material wealth above all else may sacrifice their health, relationships, and inner peace. The equation goes a bit like this:

We chase more to feel enough, and the more we chase, the emptier we feel.

The societal pressure to "keep up" creates a cycle of comparison and inadequacy, trapping many men in a race they never truly chose, with old tactics now amplified by modern technology. Buffett never bought the myth. He drives a modest car, lives in the same house he bought in 1958, and avoids spectacle. He's not playing to win applause; he's playing to live free.

Redefining success as an Omega Man isn't about having more or less; it's about being who you really are. Success means more honesty, backed by actions and behaviors supported by an intention. It means aligning your goals with your values. And it means shifting from the outer scoreboard to the inner one — from trophies to truth.

Buffett refers to this as the "inner scorecard". It's not about what the world says you are, but about what you know you are when no one's looking. Let's be clear: this isn't a call to indulgence. Happiness isn't about marshmallows and mood boards. It's a mindset that directs attention to meaningful, long-term fulfillment rather than temporary gratification that is driven by outdated Darwinian instincts or childhood programming.

Research supports this as well – men who focus on presence, values, and meaning, rather than validation, are healthier, more fulfilled, and more successful by every metric that matters. Research conducted by Van Tongeren et al. (2016)[1] found that men with a strong sense of meaning and purpose reported lower levels of anxiety, depression, and loneliness while also exhibiting increased resilience and emotional well-being. And Warren Buffet agrees!

Instead of exhausting energy trying to become the "bigger peacock," men should redirect their focus toward fulfillment and self-alignment. When a man shifts from performance to presence, from status to substance, he starts to feel peace. And peace is the real win.

But it's not automatic. Our Darwinian instincts don't vanish; they still whisper in the background – compete, dominate, conform. We can't erase our biology — but we can rise above it. We can act from awareness, not autopilot. This is when we become powerful: when we choose our next move rather than being programmed into our next potential blunder.

Buffett and Schweitzer both agree that real success is rooted not in the mere appearance of external achievements but in cultivating a deep sense of purpose. But this redefinition takes courage to step off the stage and go inward.

The role of purpose

Purpose should be looked at as the North Star. It's the guiding force that gives life meaning and direction. Without it, success is just movement without meaning. When you know your purpose, you stop chasing approval and start channeling energy towards growth. When your energy aligns with your values and purpose, your choices become sharper, and something incredible happens – fulfillment rises, and

---

References

1. Van Tongeren, D.R., Hook, J.N., Davis, D.E., & Aten, J.D. (2016). Meaning in life as a buffer against stress in men: Implications for psychological health. Psychology of Men & Masculinity, 17(3), 255–264.

validation fades. Viktor Frankl, summarizing Nietzsche, put it best: "Those who have a 'why' to live can bear almost any 'how.'" Purpose is what makes pain survivable and life meaningful.

As described in *Sapiens: A Brief History of Humankind* by Yuval Noah Harari[2], for centuries, long before Homo sapiens achieved cognition, we were creatures of instinct – survive, mate, repeat. Harari explores and tracks this, discovering that, for most of history, the concept of purpose wasn't a prevailing idea; only survival was. However, cognition gave us a choice. And that choice is purpose.

No longer must we live to survive; we can live for something greater. Robert Byrne summed it up: "The purpose of life is a life with purpose." But what is the purpose? We'll explore this in depth in later chapters, but for now, let's define it simply as a purpose that drives behavior beyond the instincts and urges of survival. It's an instinctual, yet consciously chosen, logical, and rational driver of action; one that removes fear in the process of choice.

Purpose isn't just a spiritual buzzword; it's backed by science. Living in alignment with purpose improves health, well-being, and long-term success. A longitudinal study published in *JAMA Network Open* (2019)[3] found that individuals with a higher sense of purpose in life had a significantly lower risk of mortality and cardiovascular events.

But biology doesn't let go easily. Your genes still whisper for you to dominate, impress, and conquer. Survival depended on it, so it's no wonder purpose feels like swimming upstream.

References

2. Sapiens: A Brief History of Humankind by Yuval Noah Harari,

3. (Alimujiang, A., Wiensch, A., Boss, J., Fleischer, N.L., Mondul, A.M., McLean, K., Mukherjee, B., & Pearce, C.L. (2019). Association Between Life Purpose and Mortality Among US Adults Older Than 50 Years. JAMA Network Open, 2(5), e194270.)

And traditional masculinity? It amplifies those whispers into shouts: "Be the strongest. Be admired. Be feared." It reinforces outdated imperatives, rewarding conformity to societal norms rather than individuality. But we don't have to obey. We are not our impulses and should not behave as people enslaved to them.

Today's world doesn't need stronger men; it needs truer ones. Strength isn't dominance. Choosing authenticity over validation isn't rebellion; it's the birth of real strength. It's how meaningful lives begin. Success isn't about impressing others. It lies in the courage to be yourself, to step away from the expectations imposed by others, and to build a life that reflects your unique identity and aspirations.

Authenticity beyond identity is the goal.

The Sigma Male (and why labels fail us)

Let's talk about the Sigma Male: an archetype gaining attention lately. I'm not endorsing archetypes. Archetypes are essentially identities. I am advocating abandoning them altogether, as authenticity beyond identity is the goal.

Archetypes can, however, serve as useful mirrors and temporary tools to reflect behavioral patterns worth examining. To be clear, this book does not recommend adopting any archetype, label, or ideology. Further, I am not suggesting that all men fall into the tightly defined scripts described by standard Beta, Alpha, or even Sigma archetypes.

Even the Omega Man, the framework I use, is meant to transcend labels. It's not an identity, but a way of being. The title of this book is an analogy of the arc of transformation from Alpha to Omega, with Omega being the last, or the end of the transition from one to ten on the "Vector of Self Mastery."

I mention Sigma here only to underscore that social scientists, like Dr. Brené Brown and others, have studied men who exhibit many of the traits this book promotes – authenticity, self-direction, and emotional resilience.

So, what traits are we working toward? They're not niche. They're studied, thus validated, yet also proven and powerful. But here's the kicker: a true Sigma wouldn't call himself one. The moment he does, he's chasing identity and not living authentically.

Real authenticity doesn't announce itself; it just lives. Quietly. Strongly. Freely.

At that moment, he shifts; he becomes Omega. This doesn't happen by adopting a title or traits assigned to an identity, but by dropping the need for one.

What is an archetype? (And why this matters)

An archetype, especially in the masculine context, is a recurring template. It's a recurring symbolic pattern that appears across history, mythology, and psychology.

Archetypes are not universal identities that all men fall into; they're projections or, rather, expressions. They're categories or simplified molds used to explain how men behave, what they value, and what roles they play in culture.

Why bring up Sigma? Studies of Sigma-like behavior provide us with valuable insights, helping us understand these behaviors and their benefits through scientific studies and data. This helps understand correlations between independent masculine traits and well-being, success, and mental health.

This isn't about trends, it's about outcomes. As men, we would be looking toward more sustainable behaviors, like self-governance and emotional clarity, which are both linked to better relationships, higher satisfaction, and deeper personal fulfillment.

Here are three ways archetypes function when we use them wisely.

Behavior Templates

They outline recurring traits – both strengths and flaws – seen in men throughout time and across stories.

Cultural Programming

They act as mirrors for what society expects men to be and how men judge themselves and others as a result.

Storytelling Devices

These are used in myth and media to portray different masculine ideals – such as the warrior, lover, magician, king, etc. – each with its own function and lesson.

Unlike the Alpha, who dominates, and the Beta, who submits, the Sigma opts out. He doesn't play the status game at all. His worth isn't assigned. It's chosen. Internally.

Let's break down the traits often attributed to the Sigma male and how they align with real authenticity, where Omega leads:

- Independence Over Status – the Sigma male doesn't see a need for dominance, attention, or validation. His success is measured by internal fulfillment, not external approval (Greatest Day Mindset).

- Authenticity Over Performance – the Sigma male doesn't act like others or conform to social roles. Instead, he behaves based on his principles and values. PsychQuest highlights that living a values-driven life ensures that actions match what is genuinely essential to the individual:

Those who live a life guided by an awareness of what matters most ... exhibit less stress, better health, improved decision-making, and problem-solving.

- Freedom Over Social Positioning – the Sigma male avoids societal expectations and stereotypes that dictate what masculinity should look like. Instead, he carves out his own identity through self-awareness and discipline. Psychology Today dated discusses how traditional measures of success, such as wealth and status, often fail to account for personal fulfillment and authenticity.

- Emotional Mastery Over Suppression – unlike traditional masculinity, which often equates stoicism with strength, the Sigma male understands that real power lies in emotional intelligence and self-regulation.

- Resistant to Manipulation – the Sigma male doesn't need validation, so is immune to social conditioning, media influence, and herd mentality. Investor's Business Daily (2021) suggests that purpose isn't always discovered but often needs to be created by identifying passions and aligning actions accordingly:[4]

> *Purpose is an active process... something you build by identifying what excites you and aligning your actions with those passions.*

The goal is to live a masculine life that embodies the highest level of authenticity – a man who moves purposefully, doesn't imitate others, and lives by his principles, rather than fleeting cultural expectations.

This isn't about mimicking

Let me repeat – this isn't about mimicking a Sigma. You don't "become" someone or anyone by copying the behaviors of another. The point isn't to act like a Sigma, it's to become someone who no longer needs an archetype at all.

This book exists for one reason: to help you reclaim your identity. To stop performing. To become fully, fearlessly, you. As that unfolds, the behaviors associated with the Sigma male will emerge naturally, without effort or imitation. Authentically.

We can use and learn from this archetype, and we can see what studies say about it and the associated pattern. Keep in mind that if you try to be something you are not, then, by its very nature, you are not that thing. Imitation is exhausting. Authenticity is sustainable. You don't

---

References

4. Investor's Business Daily Staff. Find Your Purpose One Breath at a Time: Investor's Business Daily, 2021.

earn the life you want by acting. You earn it by being authentically yourself.

Vulnerability as a superpower

What's the invisible thread tying all these men together? What trait keeps surfacing beneath the data? At their core, they exude and express vulnerability, something rarely associated with traditional masculinity yet central to true strength.

Let's strip it down. Vulnerability, in the context of this book, is not weakness. It's exposure to a perceived weakness with intent. It's saying the thing that costs you something. The truth that shakes. The confession that doesn't flatter.

Einstein put it best:

The true value of a human being can be found in the degree to which he has attained liberation from the self.

Vulnerability is liberation. This means that true strength is found in freeing ourselves from the ego and the constructed identity that fears judgment and weakness so we can step into who we truly are.

Vulnerability is when you have a feeling deep inside you, a feeling of fear, that you cannot possibly express. It's the fear that exposing this part of yourself might be seen as less than capable, less respected, or less worthy. It's the fear that someone will judge, laugh, or potentially diminish your value as a man.

We often refer to vulnerability as feeling or being in a place of weakness. Admitting a mistake, admitting failure, or admitting weakness is a vulnerable feeling. To overcome this, being vulnerable means speaking your truth and saying the tricky thing. This takes strength.

Vulnerability saved me

I've lived this. When I lost my company, my house, and everything that felt like "me" during my divorce, vulnerability wasn't a concept, it was my only lifeline. I had to confess my failures to my family, my kids, and my colleagues, but most brutally, to myself.

We trick ourselves into thinking silence protects us. That dodging the truth preserves respect because deep down, we believe truth makes us look "less fit" – less capable, less Alpha, less desirable.

I didn't need to run around yelling, "I'm a loser and lost everything." However, I did need to tell others – to admit vocally what needed to be said. This meant I had to have the courage and strength to be vulnerable, to say what needed to be said, and to answer questions honestly – no matter how weak, foolish, or stupid it made me look. It was the only real way I had to stop lying to myself.

Fear is afraid of itself.

The feeling of vulnerability, i.e., fear, is your body's way of telling you that sharing a weakness could be dangerous.

The fear?

Someone will see your wound and call it a weakness. Your mistake will make you unworthy. You'll drop in the social ranking to the opposite of "fittest".

So, wired for survival, your ancient brain kicks in. Instinctively, it pumps fear through your body to protect you, or, more likely, to save you from a sabre-toothed tiger.

When this fear arises, we hesitate, convinced that showing vulnerability will make us appear "less than". But this is a trap; it's fear that keeps us weak, not vulnerable. Whereas, in fact, it's being vulnerable that breaks fear's grip.

To be vulnerable, to speak the truth you're most afraid of, is to grab fear by the collar and walk through it. That's power. That's real strength.

Let's call it what it is: when you act to avoid fear, you're not being authentic. You're just being strategic in disguise. Vulnerability is fear –

but not fear of danger, fear of judgment. Fear that someone will see your truth and decide you're less.

It's really just a perception, or a guess, on our behalf that sharing creates the feeling that will make us appear weak. But here's the kicker: you only fear they'll think it because, deep down, you already believe it. It's our perception of ourselves that we think others might see, and so we want to hide it.

We begin to contemplate not sharing so we can be someone else and present a version of ourselves that doesn't have this perceived weakness. That way, no one can call us weak because we've already silenced the voice inside that's doing it.

In doing so, however, we pretend to be something we're not. We're not sharing who we really are by withholding a reality about ourselves due to fear. We call it strength, but it's just hiding.

The second lie? We act based on a script we assume others are reading. Why do we think they'll believe this act is 100% based on our understanding of what society, our childhood programming, or past experiences tell us might happen?

We rarely admit this, but the judgment we fear is just our own voice, but disguised. If we didn't already believe something negative about ourselves, we wouldn't fear that others would see it, too. The only reason someone's opinion has power over us is that, deep down, we're afraid they might be right.

But is it the truth, or is it just a mirror reflecting the fears we haven't faced? It's so wild! Every time we step into vulnerability, people think we're strong; yet still, we hesitate. Why? Because vulnerability feels like death to our old brain. That primal wiring views such raw exposure as a threat.

Even when we know vulnerability earns respect, we're still unable to show it. Often, we just freeze.

Being vulnerable and sharing what makes us afraid of being judged is a powerful act. It's so powerful that you'll become invincible if you do it often and keep practicing it – not because people stop judging, but because it stops owning you and your choice to share.

You become so "okay" with sharing your weaknesses, knowing you cannot control judgment and that hiding fear still allows the fear to exist. That's invincibility. And that's the threshold – when outside validation loses its grip, and you live unchained and free from fear.

Lao Tzu said:

> *When you stop comparing yourself to others, you become your best self.*

Not your toughest. Not your richest. You're most authentic.

Imagine what it would feel like if you could say the hard thing, no matter how terrifying it felt? To be that honest. That accountable. That strong. This isn't about oversharing. You don't need to announce your embarrassing doctor's visit to the world. But if you did something – good or bad – imagine having the courage to say it without shame. To own it without shrinking and without the inner critic screaming, "You're less now."

That feeling – the tightness in your chest, the fear of being seen – is often what makes us pretend. It's why we become someone else. (You saw this in Chapter 5.)

This feeling of fear often rationalizes what we did. Or we retrofit things – exaggerate, fabricate, obfuscate, or parrot our way out of the truth – to avoid the discomfort that can come with sharing vulnerable events every day.

Our psyche does this automatically, as our ego controls our perception to prove we're still "fit". That we still belong. Our animal side, the one at the end of the Vector of Self-Mastery, clings to repetition, predictability, and control – for safety. We tend to avoid vulnerability the same way we avoid a snake – as if it could kill us. And it can – because of our programming.

But, on the human spiritual side of the vector, avoidance doesn't keep us safe. It keeps us stuck.

This is what people often refer to as scripts. If you don't change the script, the story repeats. It did for me. I didn't even know I was reading, let alone living, a script until it repeated itself so perfectly I couldn't ignore it.

When it's time to speak, vulnerability is the first step to breaking the pattern. It's the pen that rewrites the script.

My unhappy marriage? That was just the symptom. The real sickness was a life lived for someone else. A script I didn't know I was following. The disease was performing. It was people-pleasing. It was simply a well-worn path I couldn't walk anymore.

Now, this is where some things come together. The thing about the "thing" that makes you feel vulnerable or that lets that fear come in and tries to prevent you from the next stage of feeling shame and judgment – that "thing" was primarily created by trauma, or programming, or even from your childhood burrow.

As a child, you absorbed the rules of survival; what was safe to share and what would get you hurt. Fear isn't universal; it's shaped by the environment. A young adult in war-torn Afghanistan doesn't fear being ghosted. He fears gunfire. And he doesn't worry about a VP promotion or a high school crush.

Your burrow defined your threats. It told your nervous system what to flinch at and what to fake.

To be raw is to be real. To be vulnerable is to be honest. To be honest is to stop performing.

Authenticity demands ownership. Full-stop. You are who you are, and you own it.

As I wrote in *The Imperative Habit* 2019:

> *The more a man exercises his ability to be real, the less control fear has over him.*

What happens next?

We'll tackle that in the chapters to come, starting here: understanding the mask, the drive for performance, and the instinct to avoid honesty and reality. Say the thing that scares you. That's the beginning of real freedom.

This is it. The line in the sand. The moment you drop the ancient tactics and step into something higher.

Vulnerability is the bridge from animal to human. From reflex to courage. From fear-driven instinct to spiritual strength.

Understanding our DNA – our instinctual internal urges that affect our ability to be vulnerable – is a significant concept. Yet, this single concept is crucial to breaking the cycle of manhood, which is a constant movement of the goalposts.

Spiritual strength transcends these primal instincts, moving beyond ego, fear, and conditioned responses to align with a higher version of yourself. It's about acting from truth rather than existing in survival mode, choosing integrity over validation, and living according to your values rather than external expectations. Let's break it down – it all comes back to two things: blame and shame (or BS, if you like it punchy).

How blame becomes a survival reflex

When faced with the awful feeling we get when we avoid sharing something that makes us feel vulnerable, we quickly blame something else. We rationalize why we don't need to share this thing, and convince ourselves that the discomfort of holding it in is better than the imagined consequences of exposing it.

We blame the question. The other person. Our parents. Our past. We blame anything except the real reason – fear.

For toxic masculinity, we blame women or feminism. Blame is armor. It feels strong — but it's just a deflection from responsibility. It feels like control, but in reality, it keeps us stuck. It keeps us from the mirror.

From the real work. From seeing what's really there – fear.

And let's be real – there's plenty of cultural backup for blame. Whole communities, influencers, and ideologies are ready to point the finger elsewhere. Anything to avoid the hard truth – being a real man starts with yourself. And that brings us to shame.

Shame – the shadow that keeps us small

If we can't blame someone or something else effectively, then we will need another reason. And that is shame.

Shame is just fear of judgment turned inward. It's the inner voice saying, "If they knew this about me, they'd leave." But it's best described as shame or self-acknowledged judgment; it's self-condemnation, as opposed to the feeling that others are potentially judging us.

We think, "If I say this out loud, I'll never forgive myself. I'll feel too exposed. Too weak. Too small."

Blame and Shame – BS. They're the two biggest walls between you and the freedom of being real.

To transcend this feeling, I'm suggesting that you look at this shameful and awful feeling in your stomach, like lactic acid when you run or exercise. It's feedback from your brain saying, "protect yourself." But staying safe isn't the goal – growth is. For runners, when the lactic acid says stop, we know that's when we're about to become a better runner. The elite.

Similar to hijacking the lactic acid to move forward, emotional discomfort is an invitation to push ahead. Just like a runner knows that going through the burn is what leads to greater strength, a man must recognize that stepping into his fear and shame is what leads to greater authenticity.

Fear isn't a red light; it's a flashing sign that says, "this way to courage." Use this invitation to tap into your inner strength and spiritual resilience to become a better athlete. Use it to overcome the fear of shame and judgment to become a better person.

This takes practice. Like lactic acid is your invitation to keep going beyond limits to be better, the awful feeling of fear to express what needs to be said or done is an invitation to DO IT!

You don't have to nail it every time. Start small. Gut-check yourself. Speak the thing. Then, feel what it's like to stand taller because of it. The first time I really stepped up and shared something I needed to say, it felt amazing. The fear was real. But I talked myself through it. I reminded myself what kind of man I wanted to be. I told myself, "this takes strength. And I want to be the kind of man who has that kind of strength." I told myself, "whatever happens, doing what's right will always be more powerful than the fallout."

It was exhilarating! It became contagious for me, and I found myself being and acting more and more vulnerable, increasingly raw, and more and more honest because of how great it felt.

Some people may have called it "brutal honesty," but to me, being honest with myself felt like I'd found peace.

There were consequences. I suffered. I took hits for saying and doing the tough things. I lost money. I lost friends. I lost parts of my reputation. But none of it – not one blow – was worse than the cost of staying silent.

I knew the power behind my actions and the power behind this practice. The power to be an authentic man. A man with a foundation stronger than an image — one made of truth. I kept telling myself, "I want to be someone with this kind of strength." And, "whatever happens because I speak will be easier than what happens if I don't."

The one that really stuck, however, was, "the truth exists whether I say it or not, so I might as well say it now." Say it, say what you need to say. I did, and the growth and freedom followed.

- ♦ Can you remember a time when you knew you really should have said something but due to fear, you didn't?

- Do you remember what you were afraid of that caused you to mute yourself?

- Do you wish, now, you could have said it?

Chapter 6: Redefining strength wrap

This chapter challenged the notion that success is solely about wealth or dominance, and offered a new model – one based on purpose, integrity, and authenticity.

When men stop prioritizing approval and focus instead on purpose, authenticity, and integrity, they can break free from the limiting concepts and limitations of traditional masculinity. The results? They build lives rich in connection, fulfillment, and peace.

It changes more than your life. It changes the world you show up in. Strength isn't domination. It isn't perfection. It isn't being right.

Real strength is refusing to perform anymore. It's standing in your truth, even when it shakes. It is quiet with a stubborn refusal to keep living a lie. You're flexing a new muscle now, the one that makes everything else work.

Chapter 7: Breaking the cycle

This is where we turn insight into action. In Chapter 7, we begin a practical guide to finally doing the work.

It also closes Part II: 'Breaking the Cycle' and prepares us to move from understanding what's wrong and doing something about it.

But insight alone isn't enough. Next, we rip off the final mask — the last illusion that keeps good men stuck pretending.

It's time to get naked. (Emotionally, don't panic.)

Comments From Brad Kearns

I think our definition of success changes when we get older. I love the epic monologue from Nic Cage's character Dave Spritz in the movie Weatherman. He's walking down a sidewalk packed with people in New York City. As he proceeds through his monologue, the crowd magically thins via special effects:

"I remember once imagining what my life would be like, what I'd be like. I pictured having all these qualities, strong positive qualities that people could pick up on from across the room. But as time passed, few ever became any qualities that I actually had. And all the possibilities I faced and the sorts of people I could be, all of them got reduced every year to fewer and fewer. Until finally they got reduced to one, to who I am. And that's who I am, the weather man."

Decades ago, I competed on the professional triathlon circuit for nine years. It was a dream come true to be able to become a professional athlete and travel the globe to compete with the best. My longtime training partner and top racer Andrew MacNaughton said something memorable a few years after we retired: "It's going to be a struggle for us to come to terms with the fact that our careers peaked at age 25, and nothing we do will ever come close to the excitement and intensity of winning a big race on national TV."

Whew, pretty heavy - especially when it was difficult enough to make the huge adjustment from training all day to sitting in an office all day. Andrew's comment may hold true on many levels, but the trick is to not get too wound up with some exotic and dramatic definition of quantifiable success. Little victories can happen every single day that can carry great significance to you. Like Warren Buffet says, keep an "inner scorecard." This also lines up with Dave's suggestions from the chapter: Value independence over status; authenticity over performance; and freedom over social positioning

I also think about this profound insight from Dr. Anna Lembke, Stanford University psychiatrist and author of Dopamine Nation: "The challenges in your life can take on epic proportions, but you don't have to get to the top of the mountain." For someone obsessed with getting to the top of the mountain as an athlete, that comment sure hit home.

Oh, I mentioned how getting older changes our perspective. Today, I realize that the "top of the mountain" as an athlete was *not* the mountain, but my own personal mountain: doing my best, giving it my all, and letting the chips fall where they may. Like any athlete, you win some and you lose some, but the scorecard is incredibly insignificant several decades later.

Okay, I totally buy into all this messaging! How about you? But I must admit, it's very easy to drift away from your stated values and beliefs and succumb to pressures like FOMO and comparison culture. I play this game with myself often: allowing myself to feel inferior to peers who are more affluent; feel envious of others in my industry with bigger audiences; or feel sorry for myself that part of my life entails shit work. Even when I understand intellectually how silly and unproductive it is to start obsessing about a distorted definition of success, it happens anyway and it takes some effort to recalibrate. I suppose when I do so, I can consider it a little victory. Getting over myself yet again!

Part III:
The Transition

Chapter 7:

Letting Go of the Mask

By now, you should fully understand that your DNA from yesteryear is what still influences many of your behaviors, and this is before cognition, and before what Yuval Noah Harari calls the "Tree of Knowledge".

This "Tree of Knowledge"[1] is a metaphor coined by Harari in *Sapiens (published in 2011)*, in which he discusses the *Cognitive Revolution*, a transformative leap that occurred between 70,000 and 50,000 years ago, where Homo sapiens developed complex language, shared myths, and collective beliefs. The metaphor refers to the newfound ability to imagine, plan, and coordinate in large groups — a cognitive capacity that sets Homo sapiens apart from all other species.

This moment wasn't just an advancement, it was an awakening one that turned us into the most powerful animal on this planet. Humans were able to develop skills and capabilities that led us to evolve and separate from the rest of the natural world. We climbed out of pure instinct and into the next stage of evolution — contemplating meaning beyond survival. The first step was becoming "civilized". Then, as we became aware of forces beyond survival, we moved toward the next stage — Spirituality. (Here, you may think of the *Vector of Self Mastery* as shown at the end of Chapter 3.)

References

1. Harari in Sapiens (published in 2011

Despite this transformation, remnants of our pre-evolution instincts still operate. As men, we don't just chase success — we chase the <u>appearance</u> of success. This taps into a primal drive, hardwired before cognition, to be the biggest, most colorful, puffed-up peacock. Darwin called this "sexual selection," where exaggerated traits evolved not for survival, but to signal fitness for reproduction.

In modern times, these ancient drives can become counterproductive. As Harari notes, our evolutionary software is mismatched with the fast-changing environment of modern society.

What do you think it means to "win" in today's society? Is it power? Money? Relationships? Freedom?

This is a complicated process in modern times.

And what if we've been chasing an outdated definition of success this entire time?

Research in evolutionary psychology supports the fact that many of the instincts we developed for tribal life — like seeking dominance or comparing social status — are now maladaptive in the high-speed, hyperconnected world we live in today. What once ensured survival now often leads to burnout, alienation, and confusion about self-worth. This phenomenon is widely known as evolutionary mismatch — the idea that traits once advantageous in ancestral environments no longer serve us in our radically different modern context. (Li, van Vugt, & Colarelli (2018)[2]; Kurzban & Leary (2001)[3]; Henrich & Norenzayan (2010))[4]

If we continue acting like the ape-man in a modern world, we will keep being mowed down by the proverbial machine gun. This will not be because we aren't strong enough, but because we're fighting a war that no longer exists.

Let's review

Let's take a moment to quickly review the main ideas we've covered so far.

Part I: Understanding the Problem

- **The Illusion of the "Real Man" (Ch. 1)**

From the moment we could walk, we were told what a real man is. Society handed us a script: be tough, show no emotion, dominate, and win at all costs. The "Alpha Male" or "Real Man" myth locked men into a cycle of competition and external validation, convincing us that our worth depends on money, status, power, and control.

- **The Cost of the Alpha Script (Ch. 2)**

Suppressing emotions, avoiding vulnerability, and chasing approval instead of purpose is a formula for failure. Men are burning out, breaking down, and disconnecting from their own lives. And yet, instead of questioning the script, most men double down, trapped in a cycle of blame, avoidance, and fear of stepping outside the box. The truth? The world has changed, and we have not kept up with it. The old way no longer works.

References

2. Li, J. Z., van Vugt, M., & Colarelli, S. M. (2018). The evolutionary mismatch hypothesis: Implications for psychological science. Current Directions in Psychological Science, 27(1), 38–44. https://doi.org/10.1177/0963721417731378– This paper explains how psychological mechanisms that evolved to meet ancient environmental demands are now mismatched to modern life, causing maladaptive outcomes.

3. Kurzban, R., & Leary, M. R. (2001). Evolutionary origins of stigmatization: The functions of social exclusion. Psychological Bulletin, 127(2), 187–208. https://doi.org/10.1037/0033-2909.127.2.187– This study analyzes how social exclusion behaviors rooted in ancestral environments may be counterproductive in contemporary society.

4. Henrich, J., Heine, S. J., & Norenzayan, A. (2010). The weirdest people in the world? Behavioral and Brain Sciences, 33(2-3), 61–83. https://doi.org/10.1017/S0140525X0999152X– This foundational article explores how cultural and environmental differences (especially in WEIRD—Western, Educated, Industrialized, Rich, and Democratic—societies) further reveal how ancestral drives may not align with modern values or behaviors.

- **Masculinity is a Program, and You've Been Running It on Autopilot (Ch. 3)**

This script didn't come from you; parents, culture, and society installed it. It told you how to act, what to believe, and what to suppress. Over time, that programming hardened into emotional armor, cutting you off from real connection, self-awareness, and freedom. The only way forward? Reprogram yourself. Consciously. Fully. Permanently.

Part II: Breaking the Cycle

- **Redefining Strength: Mastering the Internal Fight (Ch. 4)**

Strength isn't dominance; it's control over yourself. The strongest men aren't the loudest in the room. The strongest men are the ones who can face their fear, ego, and pain without running from it. Real power comes from emotional intelligence, adaptability, and self-mastery, not from pretending to be anything, let alone untouchable.

- **The Masks We Wear (Ch. 5)**

Every man has a mask — a version of himself designed to impress, protect, and survive. These masks come from childhood programming, birth order, and life experiences. They all shape how we think, act, and react. But masks aren't who you are; they are who you've been conditioned to pretend to be. The first step to freedom is seeing the mask and having the courage and skills to remove it.

- **The First Steps to Breaking Free (Ch. 6)**

The real enemy isn't the world, society, or other men; it's the invisible programming running in the background of your mind. Awareness is the first weapon — seeing how fear, ego, and external validation dictate your actions. From there, you have a choice: keep following the script or tear it up and start writing your own.

Preparing for Part III: The Playbook

Understanding the problem isn't enough. Now that you can see the cycle, you can also see how deeply it runs. However, awareness alone won't change your life; action will.

Part III is where everything shifts. No more theory or analyzing what's wrong; this is about execution. This is where you break free from the script and start rewriting yourself.

Here's what's coming:

- **From Awareness to Action**

Now that you see the system for what it is, how do you dismantle it? How do you rebuild yourself on your terms?

- **Practices, Tools, and Challenges**

This isn't just philosophy; it's practical. The Playbook is filled with fundamental exercises and daily disciplines designed to rewire your mindset and behaviors permanently.

- **The Omega Man's Path**

The world tells you there are only two roles: Alpha or Beta (with an emerging Sigma). But there's another option, no role at all: the Omega. The man who stands apart, on his own terms, without a mask, and without an archetype. This is the path that separates you from the noise.

- **A New Masculinity Model**

Forget chasing someone else's blueprint. You'll learn how to create your own archetype, free from the labels and limitations society forces on you.

- **Mastering Masculinity on Your Terms**

Strength and vulnerability. Power and humility. Leadership and surrender. Mastery isn't about choosing one; It's about knowing how to wield both and when to wield it.

This is where the real work begins.

- **Pitfalls of Thought are Still Pitfalls**

Obstacles aren't just things that appear in your way; they are how you see the world. The goal is to be aware of things that prevent us from our own authenticity. What common pitfalls can thwart our efforts towards removing the mask and being authentic?

For now, though, let's move on ...

Recognizing victimhood

Victimhood is just blame wrapped in self-pity, and it is one of the most significant obstacles to awareness, authenticity, and growth. It is also an emotion that supports the shortcut, "*let's do things as we always have; put on a mask.*" Let's face it: when we're scared, it's easy to fall back on what we know. For example, how tough is a diet when you're stressed or tired?

Victimhood and blame are momentary states of mind, but when they take hold, especially during challenge or discomfort, they can, and often do, sabotage everything. They rob you of motivation, discipline, and the ability to keep the promise you made to yourself. With its blame, but also with its self-induced sympathy, victimhood creates a mental trap that justifies excuses and rationalizes weak behavior. At times, self-victimhood (because all victimization is ultimately self-inflicted), can slide into pathetic self-sympathy, allowing a person to stay stagnant even longer.

I get it. It's hard. It's difficult to be hard on yourself. It's difficult to overcome tough stuff, like programming. As tough as beating fatigue when exercising. However, growth will only be as hard as the resistance inside you. The tougher the opponent, the tougher the fight, right?

And in this battle, your opponent is yourself.

The enemy is making this difficult; it's not the world, and it's not other people. It's you. It will be as tough as you are on yourself. The harder this feels, the stronger the part of you that resists change is. Which part of you is stronger — the part that wants to grow or the part that wants to stay the same?

The prison of thought

All emotions and mental struggles are just thoughts — but thoughts feel real. They can become barriers, cages, prison bars, or even swords that attack us from the inside. We convince ourselves we're stuck, can't move forward, and that things are beyond our control.

Think about the pain that thoughts can inflict. The worry about the future, the regret of the past, and the feeling that we have been wronged — they are still just thoughts. Have you ever seen someone spiral into anxiety over a medical test before they even receive the results? Their minds race, playing out the worst-case scenarios, convinced the worst is already happening.

Their suffering is real, but the cause is a thought.

I saw this happen with my own mother. One day, she told me she was cleaning her closet. When I asked why, she said she thought she had cancer and was going to die. She didn't want people to judge her because of her messy closet after she was gone.

I said, "Mom, you don't even know if you have cancer yet." But it made no difference; she was in full panic mode, thinking only of the worst possible result — she was going to die.

And what happened? Her test came back negative.

All that stress, the pain, and the wasted energy — it was all for nothing. Her feelings were real. The prison was real. The pain was real. But the reality was unsubstantiated; it was all created by her thoughts.

What if the test had been positive? The suffering would have been the same because it wasn't the diagnosis that hurt her; it was her thoughts.

So here's the truth: you build the prison.

And the worst part — or the best, depending on your response — is that you hold the key.

The cycle of fear and blame

Fear creates blame, and blame prevents growth. Your brain's only job is survival. It doesn't care about success, fulfillment, or evolution. It only knows how to react to threats, real or imagined.

When it doesn't know what to do, it shifts discomfort elsewhere. Into victimhood. Into blame. Into rationalization and excuses. It happens so fast that most people don't even see it.

We've all seen and felt shame before:

- *"It's not my fault."*
- *"That person screwed me over."*
- *"What am I supposed to do now?"*

Every single one of those thoughts is converted into a cage. It's your mind choosing blame over action. Most people never escape it. They let time dissolve one excuse, only to create another. They let fear drive their choices and call it logic. They stay inside the prison because it feels safer than freedom. Mostly, however, they're not aware that, although their feelings are real, they're often not true — plus, they're just thoughts.

Imagine we were talking at lunch, having a tense chat, and I said, "hold on. Sit still. I'm going to have some thoughts that I'll try to hurt you with." Do you think my thoughts would hurt the other person?

Of course, they wouldn't — we only hurt ourselves with our thoughts. But, here's the thing — you don't have to let your thoughts hurt you.

The battle in your mind

The average person has approximately 70,000 thoughts per day. How many of your thoughts are keeping you stuck? How many gut checks have you had to deal with fear at any level? How many of your thoughts tell you "I can't" instead of "I will"?

Most people never stop to question their thoughts. And by doing so, they accept their thoughts as reality. They react to their thoughts without realizing they have a choice to determine if those thoughts are based on subjective measures or a higher level of objective reality. They don't realize that their thoughts are based on individualized programming, and awareness is the first weapon against them.

This is why we grab that small moment in time — the one between stimulus and response. That moment is everything.

Without awareness, you react. You get pulled into blame, victimhood, and the same patterns that have trapped you before.

With awareness, you see the trap before you step into it. Heavy, unchecked emotions turn thoughts into bars. But they lose their power when you recognize them for what they are.

Let's return to my mom for a second. When she panicked, convinced she was going to die, I told her I believed she did not have cancer and that the test results would be negative. I also told her I felt her issues stemmed from stress.

She said, "I don't have any stress, David!"

I reminded her what stress was. "Mom, you're cleaning your closet, so you don't get judged after death. That's called stress."

Her thoughts were what created the real pain, even though the pain wasn't based on reality. Not only that, but she hadn't considered the fact that her thoughts had created all this stress. How could she think she wasn't stressed? Ultimately, all her suffering and all the waiting were completely unnecessary.

If she had actually been diagnosed with cancer, I'm sure a whole new level of mental agony — a storm of thoughts turning into sharp, painful swords — would have hit her. And those thoughts, too, wouldn't rationalize about what was coming next.

The truth is that fear and pain weren't protecting her from anything. They weren't making her any more prepared.

What would happen was always an unknown, just like the test results. The fear and pain were just her DNA at work; ancestral instincts designed to keep her alive. Her brain was reacting the only way it knew how by finding control, even when nothing was to be done. It helped her cope with the thoughts.

Here's the truth: fear won't help cure cancer. It won't change reality. Some studies even suggest that chronic stress itself can contribute to cancer or other illnesses. *(For the record, there are no known cases of cancer in antiquity; they did not have the kind of stress we have today.)*

Yet your brain and its Darwinian urges cannot see past the effects of fear and pain. It reacts because that's all it knows how to do. It creates fear. It generates pain. It throws you into survival mode. It hijacks your thoughts, floods your body with emotion, and convinces you that something is wrong.

And then? It panics because fear hurts, and the brain hates discomfort. Your brain is afraid of feeling fear. It actually creates fear to avoid other forms of fear. It scrambles. It does whatever it can to release the pressure. It looks for an enemy. It creates victimhood. It searches for something to blame.

For a moment, it works. Blame distracts you from the real fight. Victimhood makes the weight feel lighter. But nothing in this process actually helps you. The fear is still there. The pain hasn't left. And now? You've added self-sabotage.

I'm saying this to reinforce how to look at fear, pain, and the thoughts that create them. These types of emotions and fears drive us, as men, to connect to places, people, and things that lead us to success, while actually pulling us away from authenticity.

They're all just thoughts. The problem is that we don't see them happening. Victimhood and blame aren't decisions you make, and often occur before you even know it.

A trigger. A reaction. Whatever you call it, it's a programmed response that fires off so fast you don't even question it. We rarely recognize the moment fear starts; it's already there by the time we feel it. Something in your programming, your past, your memories, and your beliefs fires off a signal, and before you know it, you're inside the reaction. Your body tenses. Your mind races. You feel it before you think it.

And then? You act. You blame. You deflect. You put up a wall. You make a move that is unauthentic and based on perceived strength in reaction to the fear. Often, these impulsive reactions screw up our path forward.

Minutes, hours, or even days later, you sit there thinking:

- *"That was a poor reaction."*

- *"I wish I hadn't done that."*

- *"But in the moment, it felt right."*

That's the second trap. Instead of seeing the reaction for what it is — just programming — you double down. You justify it and replay it in your head, rewriting the past to make yourself right. Then suddenly, you start thinking.

- *"That bastard did this to me."*

- *"This is their fault."*

- *"What am I supposed to do now? Everything is f**ed up."*

You feel like you're fighting back as you rationalize that you should. But you're not. You're just reinforcing the same cage. Some people never stop reinforcing it.

Do you want to be this person who lets time dissolve one excuse, only to create another? Do you want to be the person who lives in a cycle of victimhood, self-sabotage, and blame — over and over again?

And if you look at the downward spiral of modern men, this is precisely what's happening. These things are taking us away from real strength and real growth. The worst part of this is how quickly we move back into pain, and repeatedly lock ourselves into fear — as if we didn't just experience it yesterday.

Push forward, or stay stuck?

Of your 70,000 thoughts a day, how many are chances to push yourself forward? How many will keep you stuck?

Consider the thoughts that:

- create doubt about your future

- make you gut-check into fear

- tell you you're missing out because you weren't there, didn't have something, or didn't achieve a goal.

It's this endless stream of thoughts that writes our script. If this script remains the same, our story just endlessly rewrites itself.

How many of your thoughts right now — in this very moment — are keeping you exactly where you are in life?

Awareness

Awareness is the foundation by which we access the higher self. Without awareness, we remain trapped in automatic patterns of thought and behavior. Self-awareness, on the other hand, allows us to recognize when we're operating from fear or ego, and thus allows us to make conscious choices that align with our higher potential. To be aware before we react, blame, or self-sabotage is the real advantage.

It's one thing to recognize a mistake after it happens. It's something else entirely to catch it before it takes hold. The earlier we notice our own victimhood, with its associated blame and self-defeating thoughts, the more control we have over breaking the cycle.

The mind moves fast. Thoughts trigger emotions. Emotions trigger reactions. By the time we realize what's happened, we've already said the thing, made the choice, and done the damage.

But what if you can train yourself to see it sooner? To dissect the thought before it becomes a reaction? That's an entirely new level of power. It's a shift from being controlled by the mind to controlling the mind. This is where growth happens. It's where we move from instinct to mastery. From animal to something higher.

Awareness is about making a different choice. A conscious choice. A choice that puts us in control. Control is a word you'll often hear in Part III.

Application of awareness

I hope that you have a deep understanding of what it means to be aware, because without it, nothing else in this book will matter.

By definition, awareness means being conscious of your emotions and your thoughts. It's the first step; the foundation of all growth. Consider this famous quote:

> *"Between stimulus and response there is a space. In that space is our power to choose our response. In our response lies our growth and our freedom."*

That space, that tiny moment, is awareness. We have to train ourselves to grab it before it disappears because once we lose it, we lose control. We get swept away in emotion. We react with anger, the need to be right, the urge to fight, correct, blame, or attack. We let our unchecked emotions take over.

And when do we respond or react with anger, or need to be right, blaming others, or even attack, we create our own mental shackles. Our heavy, unfiltered emotions turn into prison bars. Our uncontrolled thoughts harden into the walls around us; yet, at the end of the day, they are still just thoughts.

Thoughts cannot harm you unless you let them. Unless you allow them to control you.

The moment my mom shifted her mindset and turned it into "I cannot control this," followed by: "the results haven't come in yet, so why react?" — this was the moment everything changed. Her simple belief helped her shift from fear and uncertainty to reason and logic, turning panic into peace. It didn't change reality, but it did change how she lived until reality arrived. It gave her something back:

- time
- energy
- joy
- acuity.

She could have blamed conditions, circumstances, or bad luck, and let the unknown consume her life; or she could have used that time to enjoy her kids, her husband, and the moments she had. That's the point — the choice was hers.

And so too is the choice yours — at every moment of every issue!

When we choose to blame anything outside ourselves, we shift the focus away from growth. Instead of looking inward, self-reflecting, questioning our mindset, and owning our emotions, we look for an escape. We say, "it's not my fault." — and the moment we do that, we lose power, even when we're right, and even when something isn't our fault.

The act of blaming is itself an obstacle. But at its core, it's also an illusion.

Blame stops growth. If we want to break free, we must make the following understanding a habit:

> *Awareness must come before emotion.*

Once emotion takes over, we lose control.

Another obstacle is our own opinions — our most trusted beliefs.

The things that define our world shape our successes and dictate what we either avoid or run straight into.

But here's the hard truth — our beliefs and opinions are just programming. By definition, they are wrong. This is not because they're bad, but because they're ours, and ours alone. And herein lies the biggest trap — thinking we (and our beliefs) are incapable of being wrong. Everything we believe is just a perspective, but (here's the kicker) we don't know how we came to believe it. We rarely do. Think about it.

If I took someone raised as a devout Christian and sent them back in time, and placed them in a Muslim family and society, in a world where that was the only belief they ever knew, would they still be Christian?

Of course they wouldn't; they would be Muslim.

This is not because of the truth. Or logic. But because they were exposed to beliefs that were adopted, and this is everything they have come to know.

The sooner you realize that many of your beliefs were programmed into you, and accept that you didn't consciously choose most of what you believe, the sooner you'll be able to loosen the grip those beliefs have on your growth, your thinking, and your future. i.e., you will have the ability to then choose if you want to believe in Christianity or Islam, based on your own real choice, not a belief that was programmed into you by your parents or someone else.

You need to become open-minded. In other words, you need to become less opinionated and less stubborn. I'm not asking you to declare anything good or bad. I'm not asking you to change your life. I'm asking you to recognize these simple truths:

- ◆ You did not choose many of your beliefs.

- Realization alone should make you more open-minded.

- Other people's perspectives are different, but not necessarily wrong.

- If you feel someone else's perspective is "wrong", then at that moment, you are proving that you're still programmed.

Open-mindedness isn't just about tolerance; it's about seeing through the illusion of your conditioning.

Perspective

Perspective comes from programming — and it can keep your mind closed to learning. What makes this difficult is that the ego, our internal, narrow-minded survivability chauffeur, relies on programming. It is in our DNA to connect and hold onto programming, even if it is useless or unwanted.

Perspective allegiance blocks the ability to see things in a new way. Don't take this too far, though. I've gone over this lesson with people, and the first thing they say is: "*If I see a red light and they say it's green, they're just wrong,*" or "*It is my perspective that stealing is bad.*" Sure, it makes sense, but it's not the lesson. The lesson is that if they are absolutely convinced they see green, then let them see green. I saw a red light. You saw a green light. That's their programming. That's mine.

I don't need to force other people to see my reality. I don't need to judge whatever is going on in their head that makes them see something different. This isn't about traffic lights; it's about how we hold onto our beliefs so tightly that we feel the need to convince others we are "right."

Needing to be right is just another form of survival programming. And this is the real trap.

I know what you're thinking — what if this isn't just an opinion? What if we need to determine who's actually right? What if the red light/green light analogy turns into a fight where we have to prove which is correct?

But what about the answer? You don't really need to determine that; you think you do because at that moment, you're not just holding a belief, you're gripping it with everything you have. You're hanging on to the belief that they need to see things your way. And to the belief that you need to correct them.

That's not growth; it's programming. It is Darwinian forces at work. To win is to survive. Holding onto beliefs and imposing them on others is part of that same biological instinct. It's animal thinking — primitive, reactive, survival-driven. If you stay locked in that kind of thinking, you're not evolving. You're just another caveman waiting to be mowed down by the machine gun.

Consider, for a moment, the arguments or 'heated discussions' you've had with friends, family, enemies, your spouse, or any other person of significance. How many of these have you won simply because you needed to prove someone else wrong? How many were about ego rather than truth? How many arguments never got resolved? How many friendships or connections have been lost? Did any of it matter? Did the outcomes change your life?

Have you ever sat down and considered any of this?

Can you see now that unnecessary fights — those based on opinions or beliefs our ego won't let us concede — are exactly what reinforce our mental prisons. Awareness is vital because it allows us to grab that small moment in the split second before we react and use it to ask:

- *"Do I really need to press my perspective onto someone else?"*

- *"Do I even need to have a perspective at all, or can I see things for what they are without attaching judgment?"*

If you can do this, that's where the real growth lies — in letting go.

Victimhood and blame keep you locked in a losing battle. But what if the key to winning wasn't fighting harder but letting go?

Movie time — Top Gun: Maverick

If you know the movie, you'll be familiar with the story. It's about grief. About guilt. About being stuck in the past.

For decades, Maverick (played by Tom Cruise) has carried the weight of Goose's death. And now, standing in front of Rooster, Goose's son (played by Miles Teller), that pain has turned into a dangerous battlefield. The tension between them is unspoken, unresolved, and suffocating. The movie was centered around this tension. It created bad decisions for both of them. It spurred egotistical fighting. And it made interactions uncomfortable — everything was more complicated than it had to be.

And then we see Iceman — Maverick's old nemesis, and now, his only voice of reason. Iceman says just four words: "Time to let it go," in which he refers to Goose's death, or more broadly, the past. Letting go was the key. It was the only way forward. (It usually is.)

The entire movie pivots on Maverick following this advice from Iceman. The biggest film of the decade is proof that letting go isn't just a theory — it's survival. The plot, which follows the journey towards these two reconciling and having the relationship they should have had, changed drastically with the words: let it go.

Did you catch that in the movie?

Do you see its importance now?

You cannot tell me that letting go isn't real growth! Even the box office knows it.

The key difference between this book and the movie

While there are often relatable points in movies, they rarely reflect real life, and therein lies the key difference between the movie example I just gave and the experience that has driven the content of this book.

To drill down a little further, in the movie, it took decades of suffering and a dramatic turning point for the character to finally let go. In real life, you generally don't have to wait that long. You don't need a life-or-death moment. You don't need someone else to tell you. You can do it right now. You don't need time to let go; you just need to do it.

Holding on is an illusion — a construct of the mind — built from the Darwinian survival instincts that are bouncing around like a wrecking ball inside our modern world. Our animal instincts were never meant for this modern life. They were designed to keep us alive — to run from tigers, fight for food, and survive immediate threats. They were not designed to hold onto grief, guilt, regret, or wounds that should have healed years ago, and yet, for many of us, it takes a crisis before we finally take inventory of our beliefs, our conditioning, and our self-imposed prisons.

Why do we wait? Why don't we let them go with every single thought that comes up in the 70,000 times per day our mind tries to trap us. There are so many missed opportunities to let everything go.

You may be thinking, right now, that it's strange to have to let things go a million times, but it's just the way it is — and you will. Unless you want to suffer for decades as Maverick did, you will need to tell yourself, over and over, to "let it go." As Eckhart Tolle[5] says,

Suffering serves one purpose. It is to teach you that you no longer need to suffer. And you will suffer as long as you need until you learn that lesson.

References

5. Stillness Speaks (2003) — Resonating Closely with Your Idea "Suffering is necessary until you realize it is unnecessary." Tolle writes this in Stillness Speaks (page 118 in the 2010 edition), summarizing the paradoxical purpose of suffering—it remains until the awakening that shows its futility "The Place That Is Free of Suffering" (Essay) In an essay titled The Place That is Free of Suffering, Tolle offers a poetic overview of suffering's existential role: "The purpose of the world is for you to suffer, to create the suffering that seems to be what is needed for the awakening to happen. And then once the awakening happens, with it comes the realization that suffering is unnecessary now. You have reached the end of suffering because you have transcended the world. It is the place that is free of suffering."
6. Hawkins, D. Letting Go

The sooner you learn this, the sooner you can implement the practice of letting go.

Each time a thought attempts to build a prison around you, let it go. If you want to let go faster, work on releasing the emotions first. As Dr. David Hawkins wrote in Letting Go[6], we store thoughts in emotional files inside our brains. Purge the emotion, and all 10,000 thoughts attached to it dissolve instantly.

For Maverick, this was guilt. For you? Maybe it's anger; perhaps it's resentment, or it may be something you don't even realize you're still carrying. The point is, we do not need to wait. We can purge now. Purge often. Purge like your life depends on it, because it does. And when you do, you'll see it was never the thoughts that were the problem — it was your attachment to them.

Let them go and melt the steel bars with courage, vulnerability, and awareness.

Resistance

Resistance is a natural part of growth.

The ego — the biological body — resists change. We cling to the familiar because it's safe and because it's predictable.

But recognizing resistance for what it is — a protective mechanism — gives you the power to break through it. Resistance is nothing more than a wall. It's a challenge. A test. It's a program you did not choose, yet you have.

Growth demands discomfort. It forces you outside the lines you've drawn for yourself. If you want to break the cycle and escape the statistics, you have to be willing to push past resistance.

This does not happen overnight, though, so don't be hard on yourself. It takes time. It takes practice. It's a battle. A battle against yourself, and your 70,000-thought army that you have to outsmart, outlast, and overcome — every single day.

But you can do it.

We were designed to beat ourselves. It's called courage — and, whether you realize it or not, it exists in all of us.

This chapter has given you the tools to see the patterns. To see the bars before they harden. To catch blame and victimhood before they take over. It has provided the strategies needed to choose vulnerability over resistance, and to shift your mindset from holding on to letting go. Sometimes, courage isn't fighting harder; it's surrendering to the truth — and to letting go.

This does not happen because *time heals all wounds*, but because you do.

Personal reflection

I've experienced all of this firsthand. There were times when I resisted vulnerability, when I was fearful of judgment and rejection. But when I finally allowed myself to be fully seen — not just in control, not just strong, but open — something changed. The connection deepened. And that shift didn't just change my relationships; it changed me. The very things I resisted the most — vulnerability, openness, and honesty — were the things I needed to grow.

And that's the lesson. The walls we build to protect ourselves are the same walls that keep us from evolving.

Entering Part III and Chapter 8

By now, you see the problem men face. You see why so many get stuck. You see the cycles that keep them trapped. But most importantly, you see how to break them.

Breaking the cycle isn't enough. Understanding isn't enough. So, what comes next? You have to take action, and this is where The Playbook comes in.

The Playbook

Once you've grasped that small moment in time — the pause between stimulus and response — and once you've started to see your programming for what it is, then what?

- You stand. Or you kneel.

- You face the world without the masks, without the armor, and without the fear.

- You rewrite yourself.

- Now you know the truth. You know the enemy isn't out there; it's in here.

So, what now? What do you do next?

That's what Part III is about. The Secret Playbook of the Omega Man will show you how.

Comments From Brad Kearns

OUCH!!!

At this point, are you thinking what I'm thinking? This book is incredibly deep, and rich in powerful, provoking insights. It can be tiring to grind through such material, especially after another busy day of reading stuff on screens. Are you getting a little fatigued yet?

Well, if so: Wake up!! This shit is important. I want you to reflect on this Chapter 7 line for a moment: *"Part III is where the door swings wide—if you have the courage to walk through it."*

You have learned so many tools, insights, and strategies, but everything becomes dilettante folly if you refuse to put them into action. How about this passage:

If you stop here, nothing changes. The mask stays on. The programming keeps running. The rest of your life becomes a slightly more self-aware version of the same story you've been living.

Does it scare the crap out of you? I know it scares me. To achieve great things in life we have to have stakes, it's just human nature. Mark Manson, author of global #1 bestseller, The Subtle Art Of Not Giving a F*ck (Dave's book reminds me a lot of Mark's book!) emphasizes this reality nicely.

It's time to not just read this book and congratulate yourself, but take decisive action to bring the insights to live. When Dave tells his powerful story of "losing everything" and battling back to become bigger and better, it's great inspiration that you can do the same with whatever is holding your back - including your fixed and rigid attitudes, beliefs, and behavior patterns.

Now that I'm done with my pep talk, I must admit it's difficult to stay on the enlightened path. I've had occasions where I interact with Dave 1:1, he processes the heck out of me and gets me focused and inspired, and then 9 months later I find myself complaining about the same shit and behaving the same way.

Ouch! This is not a good deal. We will continue to face challenges and struggles throughout life, but we cannot backslide. We owe it to ourselves and everyone who supports us to try and grow and become better from life experience. Otherwise, we'll become:

"A slightly more self-aware version...."

What a horrific booby prize! Let's demand something different starting right now and for the rest of your life.

Chapter 7 — Letting Go of the Mask wrap

If you've really been reading—not just scanning words but letting them land—you shouldn't be the same man you were in Chapter 1. Back then, you might have still believed the old script: that manhood was toughness without feeling, victory without vulnerability, achievement without purpose.

- Have you started to see the truth?

- Have you questioned the script you were handed?

- Have you recognized the masks you wear—and noticed when you put them on?

- Have you caught yourself in moments of blame, victimhood, and ego—and, maybe for the first time, seen them for what they are: programming, not identity?

This isn't theory. This is the start of change. Even if it's small, even if it's messy, you've begun the work.

We've walked through the illusion of the "Real Man," the cost of the Alpha script, the autopilot programming you didn't choose, and the masks you've carried for decades. You've learned that real strength is mastering the fight within—not dominating the world outside you. You've seen that awareness is your first weapon. And you've learned how to catch yourself before you lock yourself in the same old cage.

This isn't just information. It's a mirror. And now that you've looked into it, you can't unsee what's staring back.

If pretending could have saved you, it would have by now. The mask is heavy. And guess what? You were never meant to carry it forever. You are not the role; you are the man behind it.

Part III and the next chapter

But here's the truth: seeing the cycle is not enough. Understanding the problem is not enough. The cage doesn't open just because you've spotted the bars.

Part III is where the door swings wide—if you dare to walk through it.

This is where philosophy becomes real-world action. Where knowing becomes doing. Where the man you've been and the man you could be—the man you want to be—will meet face to face.

If you stop here, nothing changes. The mask stays on. The programming keeps running. The rest of your life becomes a slightly more self-aware version of the same story you've been living.

But if you keep going? You'll start building a life that doesn't need the mask at all. I call this Masculine Freedom, a way of living where you no longer perform for the world but live fully as yourself. You'll learn the practices, tools, and daily disciplines to rewire the deepest parts of your identity so you can stand without the armor, lead without the ego, and live without the constant need to perform.

This isn't just the next chapter. It's the turning point. The moment you decide whether this was just a book you read or the line in the sand where you became someone new. Your true self.

Chapter 8:

Why It's Worth it

My dear friend Dave Politi was an Omega. He was a ghost in a world obsessed with labels. He didn't climb the social hierarchy; he walked around it. He didn't fight for dominance; he existed fully, unapologetically, on his own terms. And because of that, most people never truly saw him for what he was: an Omega.

For centuries, men have been told they must be either Alpha or Beta — leaders or followers, winners or losers. And then came the Sigma, the lone wolf who technically plays by his own rules, even though he is still playing the game, and is defined by the system he claims to reject.

The Omega? He doesn't play at all. He builds his own path, free from comparison. Free from validation. And free from anyone else's definition of what it means to be a man.

Important note: *Alpha, Beta, Sigma, and all archetypes (for that matter) are broad descriptions of behavior, not definitions of who you are. These labels aren't meant to box you in or define anyone you know. My reason for using them is simple: they help us examine behavior through the lens of scientific study, social trends, and cultural patterns. The ultimate goal is to raise awareness of these roles, so we transcend them altogether.*

Definition of the Omega Man

The Omega Man represents a modern form of masculinity that embodies a man who rejects archetypes and hierarchies, embracing authenticity, self-mastery, and purpose-driven living. Unlike the Alpha (who seeks dominance and leadership) or the Beta (who conforms and follows), the Omega Man operates outside the hierarchy altogether, forging his unique path and belonging to no archetype.

Key traits to help understand the path of an Omega Man

- **Autonomous:** He is self-reliant and does not seek external validation.

- **Purpose-driven**: He is guided by his inner compass, not societal pressures or expectations of purpose, embodying the phrase, "the purpose of life is that life has purpose."

- **Emotionally disciplined:** He masters his emotions and vulnerabilities without suppressing them.

- **Rejects toxic competition:** He does not compete for power, status, or approval. He creates his path.

- **Balanced strength:** He embodies power and vulnerability, knowing that true strength is self-awareness, and converting control into choice, rather than dominance or force.

- **Spiritual or philosophical depth:** He is often deeply introspective, valuing knowledge, growth, and meaning over material success, as Dr. David Hawkins would call it, 'Power' in his landmark book Power vs. Force.

Who are the Omega Men?

Think of people like Dr. Martin Luther King, Gandhi, George Washington, Leonidas of Sparta, and all the 'no-names' whose names you won't find in a history book, yet they stand on the right side of history. Think of people like the person down the street, the unsung hero in a military platoon, the brother who leads his sister, or the sister who leads her brother. Think of the people who defy the traditional roles of age and social position to remain steadfast to ideals of goodness, humility, and compassion — without the need for gain, stature, wealth, or validation.

Men have been handed a narrow spectrum of identities — Alpha, Beta, Sigma, Lone Wolf, Nice Guy, Protector, Provider; and none of them truly match how modern men live, love, or grow. These are costumes, not identities. What's missing isn't another mask. What's missing is a *path*. And while the idea of dropping our masks goes back to ancient Greece, that wisdom has never been more relevant than it is today.

For thousands of years, storytellers have returned to the figure of Odysseus not because he was the strongest hero, but because he was the most evolved. He survives where others fall because he leads with awareness instead of aggression, humility instead of ego, and strategy instead of bravado. Joseph Campbell saw *The Odyssey* as one of the clearest expressions of the Hero's Journey, but Odysseus also reveals something deeper: he is an ancient embodiment of the Omega path. His trials force him to shed pride, confront himself, and return home transformed — not more dominant, but more conscious. With Christopher Nolan's upcoming film adaptation of The Odyssey bringing this story back into the spotlight, the deeper message becomes hard to miss: Odysseus wasn't performing masculinity — he was evolving beyond it.

"In the Odyssey you'll see three journeys. One is that of Telemachus, the son, going in quest of his father. The second is that of the father, Odysseus, becoming reconciled and related to the female principle in the sense of male-female relationship, rather than the male mastery of the female that was at the center of the Iliad. And the third is of Penelope herself, whose journey is ... endurance."

— Joseph Campbell

This is the heart of the Omega archetype: a man who grows through consciousness instead of competition. Not softer, not weaker, simply wiser. A man who stops chasing identity and starts becoming himself. In the pages ahead, we'll break down the traits that shape this transformation and show how any man can step out of the roles he inherited and into the life he was meant to live.

The Omega Man vs. other masculine archetypes

Archetype	Mindset	Social Role	Primary Motivation
Alpha Male	Dominant	Leader, Competitor	Power, Status
Beta Male	Submissive	Follower, Conformer	Approval, Acceptance
Sigma Male	Independent	Lone Wolf, Outlier	Self-Sufficiency
Omega Man	Self-Mastered	Outside the Hierarchy	Purpose, Freedom

Why the Omega Man is the future of masculinity

Masculinity has long been measured by dominance, hierarchy, and external validation. The Alpha fights for power. The Beta seeks acceptance. The Sigma walks alone. But the Omega Man? He does something radically different, and he transcends the hierarchy altogether.

The Omega Man isn't defined by competition but by internal fulfillment and mastery. He isn't concerned with proving himself to the world because he's already proven himself — to himself.

Unlike traditional masculinity, which relies on validation through status, wealth, or conquest, the Omega Man is untethered. His success is measured not by what he gains but by what he becomes. He does not perform masculinity. He lives it on his terms.

As much as I try to remember this, and my thoughts and experiences grace these pages, I too catch myself hoping someone will notice — I need to remember as well. It is in those moments I call on the Omega man as a pathway, and an invitation to say, "hope is not sustainable, but just the trap that perpetuates the illusion."

The Omega Man is the last evolution of masculinity. He is the one who breaks free from all outdated "real man" scripts and builds a life of self-mastery, balance, and purpose. He's a warrior and sage. He embodies strength and wisdom, action and reflection. Self-mastery is used to move higher up the Vector of Self-mastery, to live, act, and behave beyond the pressures of DNA, animalistic urges, and societal statutes. And it's used to know that living and surviving is based on one's power of self-mastery, and not the power to copy better than anyone else.

In a world where men are searching for something deeper, the Omega Man is the way forward.

Dave Politi led an unconventional life. In Campbell's mythic language, Dave was a quiet hero. He never sought a sword, never slayed dragons, and never asked for applause. He did, however, cross into the unknown, live authentically, and return again and again — not with trophies, but with truth. His life was a quiet revolution.

I met him when I moved into third grade, leaving behind my friends and my familiar life. I'd been forced to burrow hop. I'd also had my school, sports teams, teammates, teachers, and neighbors ripped from me and had been dropped into a foreign place where I had no exposure to programming in which to succeed. I was shy, scared, and out of my element.

Dave was one of the most popular kids in school, so what made him take in the shy, awkward new kid, especially given that he likely knew full well how that kind of move was social suicide? Who knows? But looking back on it now, knowing what I know now and knowing Dave, it's obvious it was because he was an Omega.

Being popular didn't matter to Dave. Being "masculine" didn't matter. As we grew into adulthood, he didn't chase the trappings I did. He had few material needs and took odd jobs here and there to make ends meet; sometimes for a few weeks, sometimes for years. For many years, he worked for my company. To him, there was no difference in personal validation between picking up a role here and there and my carrying the title of founder and president. He lived with humility and without the need for external validation, while I dragged the weight of external validation like a chain around my neck.

Many people doubted Dave's seriousness in life. Many saw his unconventional approach to life as anything but ambition. I simply came to know his approach as ... Dave. He was just the popular kid who sacrificed his social status to save me from mine.

As a child, those experiences saved me socially and in many other ways. And when he came in and out of odd jobs over the years, that was just Dave. Never once did I judge him. Never once did I even ask why.

It wasn't until his death — an accident — that I was forced to look inward to search for answers. I asked myself why my life had turned out so badly, while his was full of purity, honesty, and authenticity.

Upon his death, many said there would be no reason to have a funeral service. His unconventional life without ambition — at least according to most people — had left him in a friendless existence. Dave stood out as an outcast in Silicon Valley, where drive and success are paramount. Not one to be emulated. Not one to be revered. Not one to even be honored.

At my cajoling, we mustered up a service for him — and what happened? Hundreds of people attended. At that moment, it became clearer to me than anything had been in years — people came to honor someone they had revered all along. Someone who'd lived honestly and authentically. Someone who'd lived life on his terms — unapologetically, without bending to others' judgments.

Wayne Dyer would say that Dave's ambition was purpose. Dave truly lived with purpose. It's his passing, in fact, that has driven me to make sense of all of this. My self-reflection from the ashes of my life's crash. And my attempt to understand what I've learned from my work has only reinforced what I now know: Dave had already mastered these lessons. Yet, he never needed to define them. He never needed to talk about them. And neither he nor anyone else ever fully realized what he was.

His legacy proves it — Dave was an Omega.

Dave wasn't just rejecting the system. He proved that a man doesn't need power, status, or recognition to live a meaningful life. It wasn't just Dave's funeral that awakened me, but my own years before, when

I'd stood at that second-story window, wondering if escape was easier than transformation. That moment was the death of the man I was pretending to be. Dave's death made me realize I had to finish what I began that day — not just survive but become someone new. His life was a lesson, even if he never set out to teach anyone. And that's the essence of the Omega — walking your own path; not for glory, but for truth.

Here and now, with your own effort, you too can create your own legacy. Although you won't be doing this for the legacy, but for something deeper — the pride that comes with the courage to live as we were meant to. To live for ourselves.

An Omega only cares about one person's approval — their own. If you put in the effort every day, you'll stare yourself down in the mirror. You'll see the wear and tear on your soul from the past ways, but you'll know and tell yourself you did it to become better, but not better to gain anything. Not for money, not for recognition, not for approval. Better for the reflection staring back at you. Better for the pride of knowing you drew from your own courage and that you saved yourself.

What comes next is the reversal of the trends; the proliferation of the Self. For that, one must have faith that others — like you, like me, like Dave, and like countless others worldwide — can be better. Faith that we can reach beyond the instincts of the animal, Homo sapiens. Faith that we can evolve into the Omega.

Benefits of the Omega

What is the real benefit of being an Omega? Let me make it simple. The Omega exists to reverse the downward statistical failures of men. The Omega helps you avoid becoming another statistic. Helps you build relationships that add to your life instead of forcing you to constantly weigh their worth, wondering if they bring more joy or suffering.

The Omega answers to no one. No person. No system. No false god of success. The only authority he acknowledges is his inner drive and truth.

To be an Omega is to be kind to yourself — not by lying to yourself or deluding yourself, but by practicing real, honest self-talk. The Omega is free of jails or binds created by thoughts.

It reminded me of one of my favorite Alan Watts quotes:

> *To take a bad situation, whitewash it, and pretend it's positive is, in itself, a negative experience. But to take that same bad situation, accept it for what it is that, in itself, is a positive experience.*

This is the core of the Omega mindset. To be an Omega is to be nothing, and by being nothing, you become everything.

What I mean is this: when you let go of the need to be seen as something — when you don't cling to an identity or a persona — you free yourself. You create space to be exactly who you are, without attachment, and without fear. That's what I try to remember.

What makes this most difficult is how often the world rewards us when we know we're not being authentic. For example, consider modeling and taking photos for commercials, or even professional photos on social media. The way these photos are often taken is the opposite of organic, real, or authentic; they are the most manipulated presentation of a person or product, and yet people (often women) are so responsive to the organic and natural look of the heavily manufactured photo.

To be an Omega is to have an unshakable belief in the power of being authentically yourself, not because you already have all the answers, and not because you've mastered everything, but because you trust you will gain whatever skills, knowledge, or strength is needed to be yourself.

Being an Omega is knowing you don't have to be perfect today, and it's knowing you don't have to be fearless to act. To be an Omega is to step forward, over and over again, despite the fear. To share what needs to be shared. To say what needs to be said. To do what needs to be done. Not because it's easy, but because it's real. It's not just feeling vulnerable but choosing to be vulnerable so often, and so fully, that vulnerability becomes your strength.

It's doing the thing even when your throat locks up, when your stomach turns, or even when the weight of the moment feels unbearable.

And doing it again.

And again.

As an Omega, you do what needs to be done until fear no longer controls you. Until you become invincible. To be an Omega is to be free from external validation, from the prisons built by thought, and from the invisible chains of self-doubt and hesitation. And if you ever find yourself trapped? As an Omega, you'll know how to dissolve the bars. Because bars made of thoughts are nothing but illusions.

The Omega lives in pure freedom from fear of thought, of action, or inaction. The Omega has freedom of expression and freedom of will.

The Omega knows that life is enough, meaning that discipline becomes choice, and ambition becomes purpose. Life is short and should be lived — truly, completely embraced. No moments wasted trapped behind bars made of thoughts. I learned this lesson at Dave's funeral and carry it with me every second of every day.

What does the Omega gain? The answer is: everything. Freedom from external validation. Relationships that are built on depth, not status. An unshakable foundation that keeps him steady while other men crumble under pressure. The Omega doesn't chase happiness. Happiness follows the Omega because he is at peace with himself.

Everything up to this point has been context, philosophy, and the foundation for what comes next. Awareness is power, but without action, power is wasted.

So, how do you apply this? How do you become the Omega in your own life?

It's time to put this into practice. However, to understand what we need to practice, and the validity of the Omega Man compared to Nietzsche, see the chart below to see what the Omega is evolving into and what it is not.

Trait	Traditional Man	Übermensch (Nietzsche)	Omega Man (Dave Rossi)
Source of Values	External: religion, culture, family, gender roles	Internal: self-created values, beyond good and evil	Spiritual & internal: higher self, truth, conscious awareness
Purpose	Survival, status, success, provision	Self-overcoming, will to power, creative mastery	Spiritual evolution, service to others, peace, detachment from ego
Relationship to Society	Conforms to societal norms, seeks approval	Rejects the herd, indifferent to mass opinion	Detached from social programming, lives in truth, leads quietly by example
Response to Suffering	Avoids or suppresses it	Embraces suffering as fuel for growth	Transcends suffering through spiritual behavior and emotional mastery
Masculine Identity	Defined by toughness, dominance, provision	Transcends gender identity, focused on transcendence	Embraces both masculine and feminine, redefines manhood through authenticity
Relationship to Ego	Ego-driven: must prove worth	Ego transcended through creation of new values	Ego dissolved through surrender, stillness, and spiritual practice
Emotional Expression	Suppressed (seen as weakness)	Acknowledged, but subordinate to power and will	Honored as sacred; vulnerability = invulnerability
Spiritual Awareness	Often absent or filtered through dogma	Generally secular, life-affirming, existential	Core guiding force—acts from higher consciousness, not instinct or impulse
Goal	Be a "real man" as defined by others	Become your own master	Become your true Self—without mask, without fear, in service of love and truth
Model for Others	Teaches conformity, legacy through achievement	Teaches rebellion, legacy through impact	Teaches awakening, legacy through ripple effect and inner transformation
Guiding Metaphor	Soldier, Provider, Dominator	Artist, Creator, Lion who sheds the camel and child (from Zarathustra)	Spiritual Warrior, Silent Master, Shepherd of Self and Others through stillness and love

The path to freedom

Most men never even get close to this level of freedom — not because they don't want it, but because they are trapped in expectations, fear, and their own minds. They are imprisoned by cages made of thoughts that are driven by DNA and the instinctual drive to be a bigger peacock, to emulate the current leader, to beat out other men, and to gain adoration. They fall into the trap of being more the human animal, less the evolved human. The Omega path is about breaking free from all of that. To move up the scale from being civilized to spiritual. But you can't just think your way into it. You have to experience it.

To be an Omega is experiential. This book is entirely about me trying to explain what it feels like, not just in theory, but in a way that allows you to recognize it within yourself, to feel it, and to embody it. I am by no means enlightened. I'm no guru. I'm not finished. However, I've failed enough and questioned enough to know which truths hold water. That's all I'm offering you: truth tested in fire.

However, I have experienced many things along my journey to help guide you on yours. My path has been one of trial and error, of learning through failure, and of unlearning what the world told me I needed to be. There is nothing special about me. The only difference is that I tried to get better by unlearning and breaking traditional methods of growth.

To ignore what society adorns as progress and the next step — whether it's money, fame, power, success, better looks, working harder, more risks, or something else. The world tells you that these are the benchmarks of success, the stepping stones to a well-lived life. But what if they aren't? What if true progress isn't about gaining more but about shedding the weight of all that is unnecessary? I tore down the establishment and went to the path of ground zero to ten. I started over — not to escape, but to rebuild something real. It's unclear where I am, but I'm here and still on my path toward more. That's the point — always be moving, never be stagnant, and keep evolving beyond what we think we know.

I wasn't always this way. I've been called many things: Beta, Alpha, and even Sigma. But here's the truth: none of it mattered. The real question was, how do I show up? How do I make decisions? And when pressure hits, how do I respond?

But before I answer that, let me tell you what goes through my mind at times of perceived danger, stress, or concerns — my practice. My practice is based on making choices steeped in my values and principles.

This reminds me of a powerful lesson from Chris Voss in Never Split the Difference. Voss, the former FBI lead hostage negotiator, explained that you can't negotiate with someone emotional or angry; you have to get them calm first.

What struck me when I read that is this: it's not just about the other person. If you want to navigate conflict or make the right decisions, you also need to calm yourself first.

This is where the Omega mindset comes in. When I feel fear, anger, or frustration rising, I ask myself: *Am I in control right now? Am I choosing from clarity, or reacting from emotion?* If the answer is reaction, I take the same step Voss recommends for others: pause and get calm first.

Because most often, the toughest negotiations aren't with other people, they're with ourselves.

I step back. I calm down. I regulate myself first so I can regulate the situation. The rule is the same whether I'm dealing with another person or with my inner voice. The one who controls their response to an emotion has the best chance of steering the outcome to the most optimal outcome. This isn't just a philosophy. It's a practice. It's not about knowing what an Omega is; it's about living it moment by moment, decision by decision. So, how do you train yourself to think, act, and move through the world like an Omega? The next chapters will break it down step by step. But let me offer a little more background before we get into the skills and lessons.

The Importance of Context

In all learning, we must first have context. Context isn't academic; it is what gives your courage shape. It is what allows transformation to stick. Context facilitates a more accurate form of comprehension.

The Transition

Without context, knowledge becomes fragmented bits and pieces of understanding without the deeper meaning to tie them together. For example, if I tried to teach you Calculus without you ever having any knowledge of algebra, you would lack the context to understand Calculus correctly. You could understand the notion of calculus, but to truly understand it and experience it, one must be able to mathematically process the proofs so its Power can be utilized.

It would be like understanding that Japanese is a foreign language based on characters but being unable to speak and make the language useful. You might recognize the symbols, even memorize a few, but without the ability to use them, they remain abstract, disconnected from real application. One's comprehension will always be limited by context.

100% of this book thus far has been presented as context to help you correctly understand what it feels like to be an Omega or to behave without effort as a Sigma. This has not been about telling you what to do. It has been about helping you see the patterns, understand the mechanisms at play, and recognize them in yourself. To have perfunctory urges, like Dave Politi, to take on the shy kid without a second thought or even to know why. To do what is right, not because you are told to, but because it is simply who you are.

These experiences must be felt. You cannot think your way into them. You must live them, stumble through them, stand up again, and do the work. And they take practice and time: patience and persistence. Because true transformation is not instant; it is earned.

Additionally, if you do experience what this feels like, it will change as your context grows. In fact, the first time you experience the freedom of letting go, in that moment, your context will upgrade exponentially, and you will have a new context and new comprehension immediately.

Have you ever done something that took immeasurable courage to overcome? Have you felt vulnerable but then expressed that vulnerability? Have you felt the fear of sharing, but then, when you did, the feeling of freedom and entitlement that you did it? Maybe not initially, but later, you say to yourself, "I am so glad I did the right thing."

Psychology has taught us that the human brain, driven by our animalistic side, is more geared to engage to avoid losing something valuable rather than risk gaining something new. We are wired to be conservative.

But that does not always serve us. Maybe on the animal side, it does, "Do I run in and grab some of that dead carcass to eat and risk losing my life from the T. rex nearby, or do I give up the idea of this carcass?"

We are wired to protect loss rather than pursue gain.

Comments From Brad Kearns

Sign me up for the Omega team, this sounds awesome! It's refreshing to even be presented with another alternative from the tired and rigid typecasting that we've been socialized to exist in, compete for coveted spots in, and judge everyone by.

Enough already! If your experience was similar to mine, you can reflect on how the mad scramble to become an alpha male that seems to start in childhood, hits a fever pitch in high school, and then lingers in the back of our psyches for the rest of our lives.

I remember when my son was involved in high level youth sports how the top athletes had an authentic swagger - even as fifth graders. This triggered vivid memories of the same dynamic happening during my youth. Some things never change.

It seems great for the studs at the front of the pack, which is why parents seem desperate to discover, hone, and celebrate their child's "special abilities." If you put any modern-day hover-parent on the spot and ask them why (why year-round soccer? Why extra music lessons? Why big dollar private college counselors?), they'd likely stammer a bit and say, "uh, well, I want him to be successful in life, to be happy in life."

Blah blah blah. Perhaps a more accurate answer is to admit how we've been brainwashed to buy into this nonsense in our own lives, and then project the same beliefs, values and behavior patterns onto our offspring. The issue is especially relevant when we factor in that deep biological drive to co-opt our child's success to nourish our own egos. This is why Stanford psychologist Carol Dweck, author of the book Mindset, and noted expert on motivation and the so-called "growth mindset", suggests that parents refrain from conveying the seemingly loving and empowering statement, "I'm proud of you" to their children. In short, the idea is to allow the kid to feel proud of himself and make sure he is not socialized to become a show pony for your approval and amusement.

Yeah, there are a lot of things to second guess and unwind, especially about parenting. We often use the term "legacy" when talking out influencing our offspring. Witness the poofy ad campaign from watchmaker Patek Philippe: *"you never actually own a Patek Philippe. You merely look after it for the next generation."* Well, you never actually own your kid either, so quit acting like you do, quit attaching your self-esteem to the accomplishments (or lack thereof) of your son(s). Complete the "authentic legacy" exercise on the sticky note that Dave recommends and start modeling that every day. Especially when it comes to parenting, actions speak louder than lectures, patronizing blather like "I'm proud of you," and even highly stylized ad campaigns.

Chapter 8: Building a Legacy of Authentic Masculinity Wrap:

Legacy isn't the gold watch or the corner office. It's the invisible fingerprint you leave on every soul you touch. The world doesn't need another man chasing trophies. It needs a man brave enough to build meaning.

This chapter was about priming the pump, preparing you for the real work ahead. Legacy isn't something you stumble into; it's something you create, moment by moment, by living in alignment with your true Self.

The Legacy Challenge: What Will You Leave Behind?

Legacy isn't a career title, a house, or a bank account. It's what people feel when they think of you. It's the ripple you leave in the lives you touch. It's the example you set—even in silence.

As you stand at the edge of the old version of yourself, ask:

1. **What do I want my legacy to say about me—when I'm no longer here to say it myself?** (Not what you did. But who you were.)

2. **If I could live every day aligned with my highest self, what would that look like in action?** Describe it. Be specific. What would change in your relationships? Your work? Your inner world?

3. **Write one sentence that defines your authentic legacy.** Not based on who the world told you to be—but on who you know you are, at your Core.

4. **Bonus:** Write that sentence on a sticky note. Put it on your mirror. Let it shape every decision from this day forward.

Remember:

Legacy is not built on dominance or Ego. It's built on authenticity, self-mastery, and purpose.

And if you live that way quietly, truthfully, fiercely, don't be surprised when the world gathers in silence to honor what it couldn't see while you were alive. That's the foundation of The Omega Man Manifesto, a new code for a new kind of strength.

> *"To be an Omega is to be nothing, and in being nothing, you become everything. This is the essence of the Omega mindset."*

Next Chapter

In the next chapter, we are going to dive into the playbook, the daily practices, mindsets, and habits that will help you shed outdated versions of masculinity and build the life you were meant to live. This is where the talk becomes action. This is where The Omega Man emerges.

If everything up to now was your call to adventure and the painful descent into the abyss—then what comes next is your return. Not with bravado, but with presence. Not to conquer others, but to become your own fire. In the next chapters, we shift from awakening to embodiment.

Coming up: How do you actually live that way? What does a life of purpose, not survival, really feel like? You are about to find out.

Chapter 9:

Learn to Live with Purpose and Freedom

We're often told to 'live with purpose', but what exactly does that mean?

When I heard that statement, I found it very confusing. It felt like an abstract idea; something people talked about but rarely explained in a way that made sense. However, I came to realize that as you learn and practice living with purpose, its meaning will evolve.

The idea of purpose is not static. It's a living concept; one that breathes and reshapes itself as your awareness expands. The man you are today may not even recognize the things that will become purposeful for you ten years from now. Please don't let purpose feel like identity confusion, because what it is, really, is evolution.

If your journey is anything like mine, there will be moments that feel like setbacks. However, they are not failures; they are moments of reflection. Moments that test your commitment. Moments that ask: Are you truly dedicated to shifting from a life driven by reactive thought to a life fueled by purpose?

Regardless, challenges will arise. There are no right or wrong responses to these challenges, only opportunities to choose how you react. I want to set the proper expectation: the path to freedom, the path to fully becoming yourself, and the path to being an Omega may not come easily. And that's okay.

This is part of becoming the Omega, and it's not a path of ease, but a path of meaning. The Omega doesn't avoid challenges; he uses them to deepen his alignment. He remembers that there is no straight line to self-mastery. There is only the decision to keep walking — eyes open, heart steady, and breath grounded.

Even if one attaches the word "spirituality" to this journey, please understand it's not all rainbows and unicorns. As Carl Jung famously said:

No tree, it is said, can grow to heaven unless its roots reach down to hell. There's no coming to consciousness without pain. One does not become enlightened by imagining figures of light but by making the darkness conscious. People will do anything, no matter how absurd, in order to avoid facing their souls.

True growth requires confronting what lies beneath the surface. This is where feminine energy often gets misunderstood. Feminine doesn't mean soft or fragile; it means receptive, intuitive, and fluid. In facing your shadows, you are not becoming less of a man. You are becoming whole. Masculine structure and feminine depth are both required for fundamental transformation.

Let me be clear: remembering that this is your journey helps. You are the hero with a thousand faces. This book — my experiences, and my words — can only serve as a guide at best, and hopefully, a spark of motivation.

Living with purpose is more than setting goals or achieving success. It's about your actions and behaviors meeting your values, passions, and what truly matters to you. And those actions, values, and passions will change because your context will. You are not meant to stay the same.

You're not failing if your definition of purpose evolves. You're succeeding. You're listening.

Wayne Dyer once wrote how a man's priorities change after what he calls "the Shift." For this book, shifting is about moving up the scale of animalistic instinct, moving from a reactive, survival-driven existence (Level 1) toward a more conscious, purpose-driven way of spiritual being (moving towards Level 10).

However, one thing is clear: once the shift occurs, your behavior begins to align with something timeless. Not trends. Not ego. Not social approval. But the truth. And when that starts to anchor you, your entire nervous system changes.

Men's priorities before the shift:

- wealth
- adventure
- achievement
- pleasure
- respect

Men's priorities after the shift:

- spirituality
- personal peace
- family
- purpose
- honesty and authenticity

Eventually, as one moves up the scale from survival-driven instincts to a higher level of self-awareness, one's actions, values, and purpose itself will shift. The things that once seemed essential will fade in significance. In their place, new guiding principles will emerge.

These attributes become the defining markers of a man who has transcended the reactive, Darwinian mindset of "survival of the fittest." They mark the shift from primal masculinity to modern masculinity, which is better suited to navigating and thriving in today's fast-paced world.

The men who refuse to evolve remain trapped in a cycle of competition, always seeking external validation. Or worse, they end up repeatedly looking for a new mask, unable to break the dead-end road of mask hopping. This path is built on the premise that the Omega finds his strength elsewhere and inward.

In this evolved state, power is no longer about domination. It is about inner mastery. The new animalistic behaviors are not aggression, control, or external displays of strength. They are inner resilience, self-reflection, and independence (not to be confused with interdependence).

Living with purpose means understanding that life is more than chasing money. Ironically, when you embody the Omega way, wealth often follows not because you chase it, but because you operate from clarity, alignment, and self-mastery.

It means understanding that true power is not about being perceived as powerful but about knowing who you are. As Dr. David Hawkins explains in Power vs. Force, power is effortless; it does not need to be exerted, demanded, or fought for. The moment you need to force something, you no longer have real power. Force is the clenched jaw, the tight grip, and the ego trying to shape reality to its will. Power is alignment. It's knowing that when you're something, there's no need to do anything to prove it.

To have power means understanding there is more to life than taking. There is giving. Paradoxically, those who live with true purpose will always have more than those who hoard. Abundance is not about what you collect; it's about what you create, what you contribute, and what you cultivate in others.

So, how do you live with purpose?

The goal of purpose is to provide direction and meaning; it serves as an internal compass that guides decision-making and behavior. Purpose is not about shouting over the noise in your mind or trying to drown out the competing voices of self-doubt, ego, or fear. Instead, it is about recognizing those voices, setting them aside, and deliberately choosing behaviors that align with the man you want to become.

This is not always easy. It requires grounding yourself in something more profound than fleeting emotions or external validation. When uncertainty arises, anchoring yourself in purpose can act as a stabilizing force, preventing you from slipping into automatic, reactive behaviors. It's meant to serve as a counterargument to the primitive, Darwinian voices in your head — the ones that urge you to puff up like a bigger peacock, to seek attention, assert dominance, or chase approval. These instincts are outdated in the modern world, and purpose allows you to step outside of them, slow down, and choose your response rather than reacting impulsively.

Without this sense of purpose, emotion and rumination can take over, acting like a thick fog that distorts vision and clouds judgment. While emotions are powerful, they are not the objective truth. They can trigger impulsive reactions that feel right in the moment but ultimately lead to regret. Many men who have not yet "shifted" operate from this mindset, and when challenged, say their decisions "seemed like the right thing to do at the time," or they emulate behaviors they assume will lead to success without questioning whether those behaviors serve their best interests.

Living with purpose forces you to challenge your automatic responses. It requires you to pause and ask yourself: Am I acting from fear, ego, or programming, or am I acting from a place of alignment with my deeper values? This simple shift — learning to recognize emotion and then choosing behavior instead of reacting — is profound.

You either live for approval or live for purpose.

I didn't fully understand that line until it hit me in the quietest moment, watching my daughter from the sideline just after her team lost a water polo game.

She was upset. Not because she played poorly — she didn't — but because she felt unseen. The applause went to someone else. The spotlight missed her that day. I could see it in her body. The slump of her shoulders. The way she avoided eye contact. The subtle edge in her voice, chewing on disappointment.

My first instinct was to fix it, to tell her she was great, highlight all the things she did right, and make her feel better. It's the push for approval — because that's what the Alpha in me used to chase: praise as proof that I mattered, and that approval could turn around disappointment.

But I stopped myself.

Instead of saving her from her feelings as I'd done to myself a thousand times, I just sat with her. I let her sit with it.

"Did you have fun?" I asked quietly. Then I added, "How you played, how you passed, how you kept going even when it wasn't your game … that's what builds your love for this sport."

I focused on purpose, not praise.

She didn't say much. Just nodded. And that was enough.

What she will carry from that moment, and what I took from it, was more important than any trophy — it was the recognition that we're either performing for applause, or practicing for something deeper.

That was the moment I saw it clearly: purpose isn't something you arrive at, it's a choice you make in moments like these, and in practice, when no one's clapping, when no one's watching, and when you show up anyway — not because it'll be seen, but because it's true.

Purpose matters more than approval.

Therein lies the daily training of the Omega man: living not from reaction but from choice. Re-aligning with purpose whenever life tries to knock you off center. Making the hard decision — not because it's impressive but because it's true.

And here's where clarity is needed: there should be a distinction between the path of an Omega Man and the traits associated with the archetype of a Sigma.

The path of an Omega is characterized by avoiding the repression of emotions. He processes them and possesses the inner mastery of planning and choice, rather than discipline to negate or suppress emotion. There's a fine line. The power and inner mastery lie in how the Omega Man uses tools and practices to process and plan a reaction, as opposed to other modalities like repression and patterned responses.

For men, living with purpose often requires stepping away from societal expectations and embracing their unique path. And this unique path is to understand the definition of purpose, as well as humility or gratitude.

> Honestly, I had no idea what it meant to be humble. I thought it just meant trying not to brag. It's so much more. It's a genuine, heartfelt understanding of how valuable life is. Humility is being humbled by how lucky one is just to be alive, and to live each moment with gratitude. Neil deGrasse Tyson has often spoken about this kind of awe, the staggering improbability of even existing at all, on several podcasts over the years. He puts it this way:
>
> "Most humans who could ever exist, never will. And so the fact you exist at all is against stupefying odds. Every ancestor in your lineage had to meet at precisely the right time and survive wars, plagues, famines, and random chance just so you could be born. The odds are so astronomically small that your very existence borders on the miraculous.
>
> But here you are. Alive. Conscious. Thinking. The universe could have created anyone, but it made you. And in this brief window of time you have, you get to feel, love, create, and explore. To waste that opportunity, to take for granted the sheer cosmic luck that put you here, would be the greatest tragedy of all. You are one of the rarest occurrences in the history of the universe. Act like it."

Understanding and reading this quote is different from living and understanding it. I learned it because Dave died. Looking back now, I wonder how difficult it would have been for me to realize this, had he not died.

As Michael Singer says in his book *Untethered Soul*: "there is no greater teacher in life than death." And he's so right. To understand how death can occur at any moment for us — to truly embrace that we can get hit by a car or struck down by accident suddenly and without warning — is powerful stuff. That's humility; not to be afraid to die, but to understand how valuable life is.

If you're alive, then you have a purpose. To live with purpose is to value being alive, and being alive allows you the opportunity to explore endless possibilities. This is the paradigm shift: purpose is the emotion of gratitude for the opportunity to be alive.

To embrace the frailty of life is an expression of this paradigm of purpose. And if you truly embrace life that much, then it doesn't matter what else happens because life itself is the prize. It's not the horrible feelings you get when someone likes someone else over you. It's not whether you're as handsome as Jon. It's not anything that puts you back into the gladiator games competition with bigger and brighter peacock feathers.

True purpose transcends competition. You're not competing for life; you already have it. You're not performing for worth; you've already embodied it.

Can you value life this much without having the teacher of death as I had? Yes! But it will take practice and effort.

So, what is practice?

It starts with connecting to these values:

Life is enough

To be used as an **awakening.** To understand that it is all I need to be proud of myself. To awaken to the belief that I am alive and working on growth.

As a daily mantra, or commitment to yourself. Use this phrase when under pressure. Say, "I will cast out any stupid behaviors that connect me to acting like an animal rather than behaving like something more than that."

Embracing these values is a higher form of humility. Humility is embracing the "life is enough" value whenever one feels down, less than something, or defeated. It reminds us that we could also not be here.

For me, beyond learning this lesson from Dave, I drew on Viktor Frankl. This guy spent three years in Auschwitz. He was starving, beaten, broken, cold, diseased, and forsaken. Yet, he led a very successful life after learning these exact lessons.

I cannot tell you how often I told myself this — 500 times a day, if needed, when I was feeling down — "I am so happy I do not need to learn this in a prison camp. I get the death of my best friend to help me learn this, not what Frankl had to endure."

If Frankl could find meaning in the middle of horror, we can find it in the minor inconveniences of our lives. If he could choose his attitude while standing on the edge of death, we can choose ours while standing in line, dealing with rejection, and facing discomfort.

To be a better man comes down to your power to choose your behavior, knowing that perception is only a misunderstood form of partial reality. To avoid faking the perception of strength is to embody real strength.

The Omega Man doesn't just live with purpose; he practices purpose. He reflects. He refines. He returns to the center again and again, like meditation. This isn't performance. It's embodiment. It's an identity-free identity because the Omega doesn't need to be identified as such; he lives aligned.

And here's the paradox: for power purposes, you'll need to share vulnerabilities. Why? Because the rest of the world is busy fluffing up like an Alpha male. Because most of society has yet to accept being a Sigma, let alone the Omega. Yet they exist. It has been proven that they are happier and more fulfilled, and they're not included in the statistics that show men are trending downward.

This path is zigging when 29 million men are zagging and following Dan Bilzerian. You will be unique, rare, and misunderstood by men and, at times, by women—the kind of women who are not worth being with anyway.

You'll also be free and admired for your strength, although few will share it with you. Why? They're likely still on the Darwinian path of animal behaviors and are still competitive with other men.

It takes a special kind of courage to counter the flow or trend of the herd, and yet it's one of the most powerful things one can do. Animals don't find success living intrinsically. They survive by killing to eat and beating the others to be the fittest.

And yet, to kill as a human is not only unnecessary, but illegal. We don't live in a society that allows us to act like animals, so let's not. We have a society built to allow the spiritual man to rise if he dares.

To live by valuing life so much that you are no longer afraid to lose it is not a weakness; it's mastery.

To live by valuing life so much that you are no longer afraid to die, through the process of constantly reminding yourself of how special, valuable, and fleeting life can be, is not a survival trait that any other animal can utilize, except us.

Not only has it proven to be the path to success, but it's also rarely followed because it represents the duality or conflict humans face between the animalistic instinct and the evolutionary civilization that leads to spiritual development. It is not yet in our DNA to behave this way. That's why it all takes practice. The "survival of the fittest" 70,000 years ago meant that Homo sapiens could not behave in any other way than other primates. But we are no longer anything like that Homo sapiens.

We are modern men in 2025, not 68,000 BCE. I'm advocating we act like it. I've come to learn, through research and my own experience, that living with purpose is not any farther away than just "life" itself. Viktor Frankl proved it.

In his landmark book, *Man's Search for Meaning*, Frankl shared that the meaning of life is that "life has meaning." Meaning is purpose. A person stripped of everything only has one thing left — the ability to choose what they believe and how they behave. To choose their attitude. To follow the path of the Omega Man means choosing to live with purpose.

Confusion: living a life of purpose

For several years, I confused purpose with a higher calling toward my vocation or job. This happens to many people. However, I also questioned how living a life where "life is enough" could allow one to support oneself financially.

Does this confuse you, too?

The balance between purpose and living

Men are often taught to prioritize external responsibilities, such as work and providing for their families, over their personal fulfillment and enjoyment of life. But you can do both.

The differentiator is the emotion — the awakening in the form of humility that comes with "life is enough," while still living a life congruent with how your society survives. We still have an organism to keep alive. However, that does not mean our thoughts need to remain in the realm of Darwinian survivability; they can depart while our body marches on.

While responsibilities are important, they should not come at the expense of sacrificing your goals, which are to grow and behave intrinsically and with inner happiness. Living with purpose involves finding a balance between meeting external obligations and pursuing this internal journey. This balance creates a life that feels both meaningful and free.

Practical steps to living with purpose

Identify Your Path

Take time to reflect on what matters most to you. This should be fluid; it's okay to change. However, one does not need to turn one's life upside down, move into a cave in the Himalayas, or wear an orange robe to effect change.

Your day-to-day life should serve as the foundation or vehicle for expanding into a purposeful life. Remember, the purpose of life is as straightforward as valuing that you are alive.

It does not mean you should be careless or whitewash reality. It's a mindset. One that allows you to rearrange your life into thoughts that keep you going in the right direction of freedom, rather than thoughts that imprison you into behaviors that only hurt you.

Understand Challenges

As the famous philosopher Sun Tzu, in the Art of War once said (paraphrased for modern times): Never fight anyone unless you know their capabilities.

It is essential to outline the specific challenges you're facing. We've all been raised in different burrows. We all have different experiences. Most importantly, all our contexts are distinct from one another. Your path, where you are on that path, and what challenges you come across are distinctively yours.

Being a "real man" means beating your demons — not the world's demons, and certainly not anyone else's demons. When you feel safe, write down what you think will really test your mettle.

I'm serious. Write down how testing your mettle will make you feel. Write down why you think it's that way. And then, write down what you'll do to defeat yourself and this list.

When you encounter any feeling or obstacle on this list, you won't be surprised, and you will have developed a script for overcoming it. However, your plan will have been created without emotional overwhelm or shame. It will be logical, well-motivated, and sound; a battle plan before the battle. Use it.

Grab that small moment in time and go to this list of responses. It's okay if you can't capture that small moment in time. It's Okay if you lose the battle. It's okay if there are personal casualties.

The response to any feeling about any of these outcomes must be that the purpose of life is to be alive, so say this: "I am alive. However bad this might be right now, I'm not in a place as bad as Viktor Frankl was, and he learned this!"

Say this to yourself as often as the battle eludes you. Each time you allow the phrase "the purpose of life is to be alive" into your mind, you have an entire army at your back to support you to try anything again.

Set Meaningful Responses to Your Challenges

When creating your list of responses to challenges, carefully review it to ensure the responses align with your vision and values. Break them down into actionable steps that bring you closer to the life you want to live, not farther away. Your responses to challenges can be anything. Remove fear. Remove judgment. Remove the perception of what society deems "a real man."

Not saying anything is still a response. Taking a step back and removing yourself from an uncomfortable situation i.e. repression, is a response. Plan your response to be free of emotion, so it is based on logic, reason, and sound principles, rather than emotional reactions to programming. Know the difference.

As your context and inner power expand, so should your list of challenges and responses. One of the clearest signs of growth is when you're able to name your demon — even in front of the person who triggers it. You're not just evolving when you can say: "I'm bad at this, and it scares me to share it, but ..." you're transforming.

To share what you are most afraid of in the face of what triggers it is the doorway to vulnerability, and this makes you more resilient. The more scared you feel when you're about to share it, the bigger the upgrade you'll receive in context and the faster the growth.

Practice Gratitude

Gratitude is a form of humility, and humility is a form of gratitude.

But gratitude for what?

For being alive. For having the opportunity to improve yourself and your manliness. Gratitude for not being Dave Politi. Gratitude for not being Viktor Frankl. It's been proven that gratitude is a powerful psychological hack. It shifts your focus and your inner voice from what's lacking to what's abundant in your life — like life itself. Gratitude helps you stay grounded and connected to your purpose.

If you can grab a small moment in time and be aware of the little feeling that takes you away from your practice, or the feeling that causes you to yell or marginalize your values, boundaries, or goals, then that is the time to use it.

Stay Flexible

The only predictable thing about life is that it is unpredictable.

Your list will help. You can update your list of challenges, but if you're caught off guard, roll with it. Rigid plans, when one feels like a failure, can lead to frustration.

Living with purpose requires adaptability and the ability to navigate life's changes with grace. It's about knowing that "life is enough." Failure is only for those who quit trying.

Authenticity isn't rigidity. It's a dance between truth and evolution. Between masculine structure and feminine flow. Your mission isn't to control the river; it's to navigate it with wisdom.

Avoid Self-Judgment: Freedom Through Authenticity

True freedom comes from living authentically. When you align your actions with your true self, you free yourself from the need for external validation or approval. Authenticity enables you to make choices that align with your values and desires, resulting in a life that feels genuine and fulfilling.

A call to action

This chapter invites men to explore what it means to live with purpose and freedom. It explains exactly what it is and the steps one can take, moment by moment, to pull this practice into your life.

By embracing vulnerability, living with purpose, and eventually acting with authenticity, men can create lives that are not defined by society, others, or perceptions.

This journey is not about perfection but about progress and the courage to pursue what truly matters.

Above all, let this land: The Omega Man does not fear living fully. He does not need a grand purpose beyond this moment. He does not require an audience. His freedom comes not from victory but from truth.

The Omega Man doesn't die early because he's not running the dying man's playbook.

Comments From Brad Kearns

"Cast out stupid behaviors that connect you to acting like an animal!" Love it! And…easier said than done. As I've mentioned in previous comments, I feel like I get into a good groove in life, harvesting some personal peace and spiritual perspective, and then a detour occurs and I drift over to feeling inadequate about my current net worth, complaining about the mundane responsibilities I face in daily life, or whatever. Like Dave reminds us often, "the path to being an Omega may not come easily. And that's okay."

It's hard work to make repeated efforts to recalibrate from ruts to a more enlightened disposition, and I feel like we need all the help we can get. I want to highlight these comments from Dave, as I think they can serve as a powerful catalyst to get your head straight:

"You either live for approval or live for purpose."

and…

"Purpose matters more than approval."

That's some pretty direct, black and white action right there! No wiggle room to rationalize your way out of facing stuff you deserve to face. "Are you living for approval or purpose?" "Um, uh, well, you see, sometimes…" No! No rambling allowed! Clean up these bad habits and express the emotion of gratitude for being alive. This is how you can quickly extricate yourself from a rut and harness the energy to take action to continue climbing instead of descending.

Chapter 9: Living with Purpose and Freedom wrap

Purpose isn't a mountain you climb. Purpose is a way you walk every day, every hour, every breath. And you're already on the trail, even if it doesn't always feel that way.

Next chapter

Now it's time to play for real. In the next chapters, I'll hand you the Omega Playbook — practical, tactical, and spiritual moves to live what we've been building toward.

Part IV:

Secret Playbook of The Omega

Chapter 10:

The Basics – A Roadmap for Sustained Growth

Have you ever asked yourself if you want this life?

Has your life been filled with struggle and confusion, making you want to quit? Most people give up when the reward doesn't come within some unknown, self-imposed time frame. They assume the path must not be working and decide it's time to reorganize the plan. This is often just the start — and rationalization — of punting or quitting.

Imagine you want to be a great water polo player, but don't get the accolades you crave by sixteen. Do you change sports? Do you abandon the goal?

Some might — especially if they've chosen the sport, or any path, as a vehicle for gain. But what about those who are deeply rooted in the love of the game or the transformation it brings? Simple —they keep going.

How many things in your life have you connected to so deeply that you're stuck with them, through thick and thin? (Truly through thick and thin!) Take a moment to think about that. Those who love to walk will walk farther than those who are walking to a destination.

For some, rock bottom creates this kind of rootedness. For others, failing a New Year's resolution by February is enough to drop the entire goal. And failure beguiles failure — meaning the goal gets harder, more complex, and farther and farther away without you even realizing.

The cycle of setting goals, trying, hitting temporary setbacks, reevaluating, and quitting is all too common.

Why does this happen? And what do we do about it?

Our ego and psyche are wired so we instinctively look for signs of survival, validation, and reward. We assume we're on the wrong path if we don't see or perceive results. We overthink. We analyze. We ask, "what's next?" We try to figure out why the last plan failed — as if the problem is the resolution itself when, in truth, it's the system we've been taught to follow that's rigged against us.

To become an Omega, you must break free from all that programming. You must learn to act and behave outside of those reactive forces, the old drives, and the failure patterns. You must tear it all down. This is tough stuff — tearing apart everything you think you've ever known and everything your mind has relied on over decades. And all of this is done while knowing you haven't ever seen or felt something better, to think that there is something better.

And here is what we often forget: the old structure wasn't all bad. Some pieces of it worked. Some beliefs helped you survive. This isn't a demolition out of rage; it's a conscious renovation. Keep the beams that hold integrity. Replace the ones that no longer serve. The Omega rebuilds, but only after the excavation.

This chapter is about pulling in the techniques needed to achieve this. However, let me be clear: nothing should be expected in return. No trophy. No reward. No payday. The reward is not in applause. It is in peace. It's not a trophy you place on the shelf, but a truth you carry in your chest. When no one is watching, when nothing is guaranteed, you keep showing up. That's the real prize.

Just a life steeped in values that match those of a free man. A real man. A man who never questions what that even means again. He lives it consistently. Daily. Constantly.

Those values, while forged in fire, are softened by grace. A man in alignment does not need to raise his voice. His stillness speaks for him. His presence becomes gravity.

Important Note: This chapter isn't where we do the work. This is where we learn how to train for the work. These seven "basics" aren't just ideas — they're the conditioning drills that give you the stamina and focus to run the Omega plays in the next chapter.

The journey of growth

Personal growth is not a destination; it's a continuous, never-ending journey. It demands commitment, self-awareness, and the willingness to adapt, evolve, and transform over time. Real growth requires stepping outside your comfort zone, embracing discomfort, and learning from every setback, fall, and failure along the way.

This applies to all forms of growth. Whether it is personal, emotional, professional, or physical, the journey is the same.

As mentioned above, sports provide an excellent teaching and testing ground for these principles. Growth in sports often gives us a concrete way to understand how progress works. But make no mistake; the path is no different when it comes to inner transformation. The formula is universal.

For me, the confusing part was realizing that the growth path in sports mirrors the path of personal development. In athletics, we're used to having coaches. We expect a trained eye to point out our mistakes, give us adjustments, and help us fine-tune our game. Most people don't think of applying that same level of observation and correction to themselves.

What if you were both the athlete and the coach? What if your inner growth demanded the same film review, the same humility to be corrected, and the same willingness to adjust?

The road to peak performance in sports is well-documented and studied. Coaching methods and performance principles have been refined for decades. Yet even in sports, we rarely stop to break down the real mechanism of growth, what's happening beneath the drills, the reps, and the feedback.

If you strip the system down to its core, the methods are the same ones I share with you in this book. This is not some radical new approach, and I'm not reinventing the wheel here.

It all starts with awareness.

In sports, your coach provides this. They observe you, watch the reps, and identify what needs to be adjusted. They say, "you're dropping your shoulder," or "tuck your head tighter." That simple correction becomes the foundation for the next phase of your growth.

In life? In manhood? In the journey to become an Omega?

You have to be your own coach. You have to learn how to become the observer and how to generate awareness of your thoughts, behaviors, and habits so you can self-correct and grow. Most men trying to climb the outdated Beta hierarchy do this by mimicking other men who appear successful. But the Omega path doesn't copy anyone. It demands awareness from within.

Next comes behavior modification.

Once a coach gives feedback, the athlete adjusts the behavior. Tuck the head. Square the shoulders. Keep the elbow in. It's the same process here. You create awareness, then you adjust. That's what the Omega Playbook is all about: it's your set of advanced tools and your internal coach. You apply it the same way you'd apply a coach's feedback in a game.

Then there are the fundamentals.

Every sport has a baseline of athleticism that supports overall performance. Do you want to be a better soccer or football player? Run more. Soccer is a sport, and running is a fundamental part of it. Want to be a better water polo player? Swim faster. Polo is the sport, and swimming is the fundamental part. Want to be a better ice hockey player? Improve your skating. Ice hockey is the sport, and skating is the fundamental part.

The fundamentals are the core skills on which everything else is built. In the journey of self-mastery, vulnerability is fundamental.

Vulnerability is to self-mastery, as running is to soccer, as swimming is to water polo, and as skating is to ice hockey. It's the core. The baseline. The thing that makes you execute the sport better.

For those who don't relate to sports, consider this: vulnerability is to inner growth what scales are to a musician, or what silence is to a monk. It's the thing behind the thing. The invisible discipline that makes the visible transformation possible.

In the same way that athletes work on their conditioning behind the scenes, you must train every single day in vulnerability. It's not the highlight reel moment, but it's what makes all the high-performance plays possible. It's the foundation of this journey; without it, nothing sustainable can be built.

Practice

Just like in sports, self-mastery and personal growth require one thing above all else: practice.

Practice is the training ground for transformation, and, just like in athletics, how you practice matters. One tip I always followed when trying to enhance my performance, whether in sports, business, or life, was to practice the way I wanted to play.

No one embodied this more than Michael Jordan, who famously said:

> *You can practice shooting eight hours a day, but if your technique is wrong, then all you become is very good at shooting the wrong way. Get the fundamentals down, and the level of everything you do will rise.*

Practice isn't punishment, and it shouldn't feel like suffering. However, that's not to say it doesn't take effort. It does. But effort fueled by passion hits different. The man who trains because he wants to evolve will always outperform the one who trains because he thinks he's broken.

Practice is how we shape the subconscious mind, which is where your behavior lives when you're not thinking. It's where real change happens — not when you're trying hard but when you're acting automatically. Practice is what builds the default behavior of the Omega Man.

Let me share an example:

A dear old friend of mine was a college All-American football player who got drafted by the Dallas Cowboys. On his very first day of training camp, his defensive line coach introduced him to a drill called "The 3-Inch Step," a small but critical movement required for linemen at the pro level. My friend, already a star in college, said, "coach, I already know how to do my first step."

The coach looked him in the eye and said, "great. Then it shouldn't take long to ensure you know how to do it at this level."

For weeks, that was the only drill they opened with — the same 3-inch step. Over and over. Every day.

Why?

Because mastery requires repetition at the right level. This kind of subconscious training is about unlearning and relearning; it's about refining the most minor details until they become automatic, and until the body and mind perform without hesitation. Eventually, it will occur without thought.

Mastery is not a repetition of variety. It's a variation of the essential. What looks simple from the outside becomes sacred to the person who understands its depth.

This is what most people overlook in the journey of growth. They want the results of mastery, but they skip the reps. They chase transformation but forget the drills. They read the theory but avoid the practice. People are always jealous of the results but rarely jealous of the effort that went into the journey.

Choose the journey, not the finish.

In sports, we call it muscle memory. In psychology, it's called programming. In daily life, we refer to it as a habit. But it's all the same:

it's what you've trained your subconscious to do when no one's watching, when you're not thinking, and when life tests you.

To become a master of yourself — to become an Omega — you have to reprogram your subconscious. And that happens through daily, deliberate, disciplined practice.

This chapter is where we begin giving you the equivalent of that "3-inch step." The foundational movements. The drills you repeat until they become your nature. Your new muscle memory.

We'll call them *The Basics*.

The Basics *(skills needed and practiced dozens of times daily)*

These are your foundational skills. Like dribbling in basketball, scales in music or footwork in soccer, these tools must be trained and repeated until they become instinctive. The more often you apply them, the more natural they become until they're no longer something you try to do but something you just are. This is how you become unshakable.

Basic #1: Awareness

Awareness is your internal coach.

In sports, we rely on coaches to point out what we miss. We rely on them to hover, observe, and catch even the smallest technical flaws. A coach sees that our chin wasn't tucked tightly enough during a dive or that our elbow was bent wrong on a tennis swing.

But in this game of self-mastery, you are your coach. And if you don't have awareness and you're not actively watching your mental form, you'll miss the little things. You won't know when to catch yourself, redirect, or tighten your posture. You'll miss the clues. Awareness is what allows course correction. It's what gives you the power to step out of reactive behavior and into conscious growth. The cannot be overstated enough!

Basic #2: Vulnerability

Vulnerability is the gateway to self-reflection. Without vulnerability, there's no honest audit. There's no real growth. If you can't look at yourself clearly because you're afraid to feel dumb, wrong, or "less than", you're trapped. That fear is a prison built entirely of thoughts.

Growth comes from facing it anyway.

Imagine if Steph Curry sugarcoated every missed shot, saying, "that was close ... I'm great because I almost made it." He'd never improve. He'd never adjust. Vulnerability allows us to look honestly, critically, and compassionately. It's not self-loathing, it's self-honoring. To see the truth is to give yourself the chance to rise.

This is the breeding ground for success in sports, music, art, business, life — and in becoming an Omega.

Personal Perspective

Vulnerability isn't about weakness; it's about courage — the courage to be real when it counts. When it is hard.

Let me tell you a story:

When I was going through my divorce, I was literally broke. *(I eventually lost my house in the fallout of this business and my choice to leave the marriage.)*

The business my ex and I had built was collapsing. We still had to chase unpaid invoices and wrap up lingering projects. She wouldn't buy me out or let me buy her out.

"The business goes with the marriage," she said.

So I replied, "Then it ends."

One of those final projects was bonded. We were barely able to limp to the finish line. The client hated us. And, frankly, I hated them. But we had no resources left, and we were about to lose hundreds of thousands of dollars. The bonding company stepped in and said, "our job isn't to help you get what you're owed. It's just to finish the job."

Translation: *You're out of luck.*

I was handed the final settlement paperwork. Everyone knew we were done. The client would keep what was left — *years* of our profit — and there was nothing we could do.

I turned to the VP of the client company, John, and I said, "John, I'm going through a divorce. I'm going to sign this paperwork. You're under no obligation to give us anything. But I'm asking — not as a contractor, but as a man going through hell — would you consider peeling off $50,000 for us? It's a small number for your company, but it would mean everything to me."

He paused. Thought about it. And he finally said, "you know what? I will. Not because I have to, but because you didn't posture or play games. You were honest. You asked with humility. but mostly because you were so vulnerable, and that deserves something."

That moment taught me something I've never forgotten: when you drop the mask, people respond to the truth. And even when they don't, you will know that you did. That is not a weakness. It's the opposite.

Vulnerability works. Not always in dollars. But always in dignity.

Basic #3: Belief and Behavior Modifications

This is your swing. Your shot. Your stroke.

This is the muscle that drives change. The subconscious mind must be trained, and it's trained through repetition. By consistently behaving in alignment with the values you want to believe, you rewire yourself from the inside out.

You can *change* what you believe. You must. Your beliefs shape your feelings, and your feelings drive your behavior. That's the loop.

Here's a personal example: At some point, I decided I never wanted to do anything just for gain again. I wanted to live from a place of morality, alignment, and purpose— not for attention or reward. That meant doing the right thing, with no expectation of recognition.

If I had friends over for dinner, it didn't matter whether they had a fantastic time or not. I tried my best to host them well. If they enjoyed it, great. If they didn't like the food, that wasn't entirely my fault. My intention was clean. I wasn't hosting them for praise. I didn't ask if they had a great time. I didn't need a pat on the back. The purpose was the act itself.

That's belief-based behavior in practice, and we must use it for the next section.

Basic #4: Self-Esteem as a Belief

Self-esteem is not some magical personality trait you're born with, such as "high" or "low" self-esteem. It's not like a permanent tattoo. Self-esteem is a belief. It's whatever you choose to believe about yourself.

Be honest: what would you choose if you had a powerful ring (not quite "The Precious," but close)? What if that ring gave you the power to believe anything about yourself instantly? You'd choose to believe you're strong, grounded, confident, and worthy. You'd choose the highest, most balanced self-esteem imaginable. You wouldn't pick "low self-esteem," would you? Hell no.

So here's the hard truth: if you're walking around with low self-esteem, that's a belief you've been programmed into. It's not who you are. It's what you've learned to think you are.

You were told who you are by parents, siblings, coaches, bullies, and maybe even by your own internal dialogue — and you believed it. As a kid, you didn't have a spam filter. All that noise slipped in and took root.

But just because it got in doesn't mean it's true.

What's stopping you from believing something better now? Only two things:

1. The decision to change your mind.

2. The courage to act like the person you want to become, even before you fully believe it.

At first, it might feel like you're faking it. That's okay. It's called training wheels. You're not faking who you *are*. You're retraining your subconscious. You're building a new mental operating system. You're updating the code.

Eventually, those actions will no longer feel awkward. They'll become you. That's when the belief locks in. Not because someone said you were worthy, but because you lived like it, day in and day out.

Adopt the unshakeable belief that you're enough. That life is enough. That no outdated programming has the power to tell you otherwise.

Believe it. And more importantly, behave it.

Dr. Wayne Dyer said, "If you change the way you look at things, the things you look at change."

That's not just poetic, it's neurological. What you focus on becomes your experience. What you believe becomes your perception. And with self-esteem, there is no more powerful quote to change.

Basic #5: Self-Reflection and Adaptation

Now comes the work of refining.

To adapt, you must reflect. As Stephen Hawking said, "intelligence is the ability to adapt to change." This requires awareness and vulnerability, but it also demands honesty — brutal, beautiful honesty.

The ego resists honesty. It's designed to preserve outward appearance by protecting inward self-image. It rationalizes. It blames. It filters. But these filters formed in your "burrow", and in your past, are often outdated. They don't serve your future. And they must be confronted and challenged if you want to evolve.

Basic #6: Compare and Contrast

Use reflection to compare your actions to your goals — not your goals of achievement, but your goals of alignment. Of values. And of character.

Did your behavior match your code? Did you act in a way that reflects the man you are becoming?

Remember, your values and goals will shift as your context shifts. Wayne Dyer noted that priorities change after "The Shift." The deeper your awareness, the more fluid your goals become, and that's not weakness; that's growth.

Basic #7: Repeat

Repetition is transformation.

In Atomic Habits, James Clear writes, "every action you take is a vote for the type of person you wish to become." Most people read that and think of performance improvement. The Omega reads it differently.

Repetition isn't about discipline; it's about alignment. It is the slow, deliberate shaping of the man you are returning to — the man beneath the performance, beneath the programming, beneath the mask.

Think of someone learning to fight southpaw when they've been right-handed their whole life. That shift requires constant awareness and constant practice. The body must create new neural pathways. The nerves must rewire. The feedback must be recalibrated repeatedly.

It takes time, patience, and effort, but eventually, you become ambidextrous. Your skillset grows. You become more adaptable, more resilient, and more powerful.

Repetition for awareness, vulnerability, belief, reflection, and repetition will allow them to become second nature. They're not just tools you use, but how you live.

These are The Basics. They're not beneath you. They're not beginner steps. These are elite habits executed daily, sometimes hourly. When mastered, they are what make the Omega Man unstoppable.

Steps for Sustained Practice and Growth

When it comes to implementing this into your life, start with seven days! Ease into it. Track your progress. Build momentum. The Omega doesn't wait for perfection; he builds it, like stacking Legos, one piece at a time. As Lao Tzu said, "the journey of a thousand miles begins with a single step."

Daily reflection

Growth requires intention, and intention requires awareness. Set aside a few minutes every day to reflect on your behaviors, emotions, and decisions. This is your daily film review, the same as the way an athlete watches game tape. What patterns are repeated? Where did you react instead of respond? What felt aligned, and what didn't? Journaling, meditation, or just ten minutes of silence can help you identify what to keep doing and what to shift. Without reflection, there's no correction.

Stay curious

Curiosity is the antidote to judgment. When you stay curious, you stop labeling yourself as "broken" or "not enough" and instead begin asking, "Why did I react that way?" or "What could I do differently next time?" Curiosity keeps you open. It allows you to challenge long-held beliefs and question emotional programming without shame. A curious mind sees every experience as a chance to learn, not a verdict on your worth.

Judgment closes the heart. Curiosity opens it. That's the feminine wisdom the masculine mind often forgets.

Cultivate resilience

Growth does not happen in a straight line. It's messy. There are days of motivation and days of doubt. Resilience is the ability to keep going, especially when the results are slow or invisible. This isn't about blind perseverance; it's about building inner strength. Practices like mindfulness, gratitude, and self-compassion help you bounce back faster and stronger. Real resilience isn't the absence of pain; it's your capacity to walk through it with grace and purpose, again and again.

Prioritize self-care

You cannot grow from a depleted state. Personal growth demands energy — physically, emotionally, and spiritually. Rest is not a weakness. Recovery is not a luxury. Whether it's getting enough sleep, eating foods that support your energy, moving your body, or carving out time to be still, these are foundational. But perhaps even more important is spiritual balance. A life that's all work or all pleasure is a life that lacks direction. Balance signals that you're connected to something more profound: your values, your peace, and your self-mastery.

Self-talk

Your internal voice is either your greatest coach or your worst enemy. Self-talk is not just about mantras or feel-good affirmations. It's the ongoing narrative you feed your subconscious mind. Are you encouraging yourself through challenges or criticizing every stumble?

Try these strategies:

- Speak to yourself like someone you love.

- Replace "I can't" with "I'm learning."

- Replace "I failed" with "I learned."

- Speak with strength, not self-punishment.

Every word you think is a brick, so be careful what kind of structure you're building. This, too, is where self-esteem can change. Make a daily habit of telling yourself that life is enough. Learn the lesson death teaches us and live it. Talk to yourself about these powerful lessons every day.

This is not fluff. This is subconscious reprogramming at the emotional level. And that's where real transformation lives below the surface, in the quiet echoes of your inner voice.

Mindset shifts for growth

- **Embrace failure as a teacher**

Failure isn't the end; it's feedback. It's a film for your next game. The only actual failure is letting the setback cause you to rewrite your identity with another mask.

- **Adopt a growth mindset**

Believe — really believe — that who you are today is not who you have to be tomorrow. Skills can be learned. Emotional intelligence can be built. Masculinity can evolve. The past may have written your starting point, but your mindset writes your next page.

- **Let go of perfectionism**

Perfection is the ego's way of avoiding vulnerability. Aim for progress. Show up messy. Try again. Learn. That's mastery.

Tools for navigating challenges

- **Mindfulness (awareness practices)**

Stay grounded in the now. When emotions flare, anchor yourself in breath, body, or observation. This creates space between the trigger and the response.

- **Goal setting**

Break significant transformations into tiny, winnable moments. Want to become more vulnerable? Start by sharing something honest with a trusted friend. Repeat.

- **Adaptability**

Life will not go according to plan. That's the plan. Learn to pivot. Flow. Evolve. Rigidity is the ego clinging to control. Flexibility is power. Adaptability is masculine wisdom, wearing feminine grace. The ability to bend without breaking. To stay grounded without being fixed.

Practices for growth

- **Defining what is real**

Your thoughts are not always reality; just because you feel something doesn't make it true. The practice of discernment to separate fact from fear is essential.

- **Meditation**

This is your training ground. This is "on the mat" training. It is structured Awareness training. Meditation isn't about clearing your mind; it's about learning to witness your mind without reacting. It's the practice of sitting still with yourself long enough to hear the noise ... and then practice quieting it. Over time, it rewires your nervous system and trains you to respond with calm, rather than chaos. This is your Omega gym. Meditation is where all parts of you meet. The discipline of sitting. The surrender of listening. The courage to stay.

- **Active awareness**

Awareness doesn't end when our meditation practice ends. Thus, "active awareness". What we learn "on the mat" is meant to carry into the rest of daily life. Some call this "off the mat"—bringing awareness into motion. It means noticing your thoughts during a conversation, observing your reaction in a stressful moment, or tracking your breathing as you walk. The more you practice awareness in daily life, the more natural and automatic it becomes.

Adaptability or extinction

Stephen Hawking once said the species most likely to survive are not the strongest or the smartest but the most adaptable. The dinosaurs didn't adapt. Neither did Neanderthals. Homo sapiens survived because we evolved with cognition, an inner awareness that allows us to change behavior, not just react.

The modern man faces a new extinction not of body but of purpose. We're no longer needed to hunt or protect with strength alone. What society needs now is emotional resilience, authenticity, and inner power. The Omega Man isn't extinct; he's just rare. He survives because he adapts.

Will you?

Comments From Brad Kearns

I love Dave's early comments in this chapter: "nothing should be expected in return. No trophy. No reward…keep showing up when nothing is guaranteed."

This reminds me of my athletic journey, where I raced on the professional triathlon circuit in my younger days, and am now trying to excel in obscure track & field competitions for people in the older age groups. Back in the day, my triathlon journey was colored by the hype of professional sports: Prize money, sponsors, television and print media coverage - all manner of carefully cultivated attention and importance.

As an integral player in the game, it was easy to get sucked in and start believing that what you are doing is super important; believing that losing a race is a tragedy requiring crisis management measures; believing that winning makes you hot shit on the planet - until the next tragedy occurs and you return to second guessing and self-doubt. This is a roller coaster ride that many athletes experience thanks to the inherently fragile ego of the athlete, and the power of measuring, judging outside influences (remember, "fans" is an abbreviation for "fanatics")

Today, I still pursue athletic goals with the same intensity and passion, but it's no longer my livelihood, nor does training occupy the majority of my days. With all the fanfare stripped away, what remains is the purity of training and competing; the pursuit of personal growth and the self-satisfaction of doing your best throughout the process. The late basketball coaching legend John Wooden puts this as the top square on his *Pyramid of Success: Competitive Greatness* - the enjoyment of a difficult challenge.

I climbed up a very competitive pyramid during my triathlon career, but I don't think I embodied Wooden's ideals as well as I do now, when the stakes are insignificant. How about you? Can you strip away outside noise and pursue competitive challenges with nothing expected in return? When you do so, you can better connect to this "journey to Omega" that Dave is coaching us on.

Chapter 10 — a call to action wrap

This chapter isn't just advice. It's a challenge to become the kind of man who doesn't just change but keeps changing. I want not just to have a better life but to live one every day through the way I think, act, speak, and recover.

So, what will you commit to?

What belief will you program into your mind and reinforce with action until it becomes second nature?

This journey is not about perfection; it's about the relentless practice of growth. And it's not about practice for your mind or body, but for your soul. It's about building a life rooted in values so strong they cannot be shaken by circumstance. The habits, the mindset shifts, and the internal playbook are now yours. But ownership is only the beginning.

Now we get into the real work: making it last. Living it every day, even when no one's watching. Especially when no one's watching.

The Omega path isn't just a breakthrough it's a lifestyle. Sustaining that lifestyle requires tools. Reinforcement. Spiritual fuel. Daily rituals that recalibrate your mind, strengthen your purpose, and reconnect you to your values.

The Omega Man does not grow in isolation. Every practice you commit to becomes a quiet offering to the people around you. Your stillness affects your family. Your patience teaches your children. Your integrity sharpens your love. You are not just building yourself; you are becoming the gravity that grounds others. This is not selfish work. This is sacred work.

That's where we go next.

None of this is about being perfect. Instead, it's about practicing perfectly and showing up repeatedly, even when you don't feel like it. Especially then. And absolute mastery? It's invisible until it's unstoppable.

Next chapter

In Chapter 11, we go even deeper into the emotional behaviors that define the Omega Man: less theory, more living, more being.

Chapter 11:

The Playbook – Spiritual Behaviors to Live By

This is it! The playbook!

This chapter will build on the basics covered in previous chapters and introduce the playbook, play-by-play.

Up to this point, the entire book has been building to this chapter. Now, you'll be provided with hands-on, direct, and clear steps you can take to build the immortal masculine life, I call the Omega — or "the last". (I call it "the last" as it is almost the end of the trajectory from Alpha to Omega.).

Ahead, you will find fifteen powerful and life-changing plays. The important thing to remember is that these "plays" are not rules. There are no rules. Plays are a belief and a behavioral structure that I call "spiritual behavior". If practiced, they will ensure anti-mask wearing and life as an Omega.

What do I mean by spiritual behaviors?

Let's return to a concept we touched on earlier — a moment in time, or a pattern you've likely felt before. I'll use my sports analogy to anchor it, and then bring in Einstein's wisdom to show what's really at stake.

The sports analogy

When we run or do any form of exercise, our mind starts speaking to us. It might be unprovoked and uncontrolled, but it definitely speaks. The mind speaks by taking orders from the feedback given by the body. The body emerges and is constantly connected to biological signals, such as hormones and neurotransmitters, as they whisper through our bloodstream. Our minds have one goal in mind: to keep us alive. For example, when exercising, it says things like: This is hard. You're tired. Maybe you should stop.

That self-talk isn't wisdom; it's biological instinct, attempting to save our lives.

It's not insight — it's survival. The rapid heartbeat, the perspiration, the burn of lactic acid as it builds up … it's enough to trip an ancient wire inside us, making the body react, and send the message: This isn't safe. Conserve energy. Quit.

That voice is biological, and so is the mental chatter that follows. We think mental chatter is us, but really, it's our mind processing the data of the exercise and reporting back to the brain. The voice is the brain trying to get us to stop.

This happens without our permission. Both the physical signals and the automatic commentary arrive uninvited. This is our programming at work. It's an inherited operating system designed to keep us alive, not help us grow.

But just as fast as that voice says stop, another voice can speak up. A little voice that is not made by neurofeedback or signals from muscular fatigue, bringing fear of bodily harm. A little voice that is not created automatically from neuropeptides, but a voice, a quiet strength created from intention. We tell ourselves:

- "Keep going."

- "This is where it begins."

- "You've got more."

That voice is not from the body. It's a choice. That voice is spirit. Our spirit.

To override the body is to act spiritually. To say "no" to the programming and "yes" to the higher path is what I call spiritual behavior — behavior that follows a choice to act beyond the feedback of the body, regardless of what that feedback is. This is where free will lives, not in theory but in practice. You may believe in a greater form of free will, as I do. But right here — this is the earliest stage of free will. To me, this is biological free will — the ability to rise above the animal inside you and choose beyond it. And that's why this analogy matters.

Everything in this chapter builds on this idea. This definition of spirituality is to go beyond the body and act on intention, to act of biological free will, maybe not with exercise but with everything else — stress and fear, and the drive to survive, be loved, accepted, felt, heard, hugged, and so on. The question is — can and will you behave beyond the unprompted voices that are pushing you to do things?

Potential pitfall

Spiritual override over the body is not about silencing intuition; it's about discerning between intuition and biological instincts. One whispers truth — intuition; the other shouts fear — the body looking to survive. Awareness helps us hear both. Spiritual behaviors give us the courage to decide which voice we hear and act on, such that we are the ones making the choice, not an automated biological being living out of programming.

If you remember this dynamic — this tension between the voice of survival and the voice of spirit — you'll begin to understand what Einstein meant when he said: *The true value of a human being is determined primarily by how he has attained liberation from the self.*

He wasn't talking about the self we brand or perform; he meant the biological self. The self that panics, chases, clings, and fears. The spiritual man — the Omega man — learns to rise above it, more consistently than not. Each override moves you closer to who you truly are.

Einstein's quote revisited

As mentioned in Chapter 2, Einstein understood the potential for this higher power — the force that exists beyond the body — and knew it was where the actual value of a human was measured. He also knew that this knowing isn't limited to one path. There are many ways to access it, but no matter how you get there, one truth remains — it takes practice. It's not intellectual. It's not theoretical. It's experiential.

Once you begin to feel that ability to act beyond your body — to override your instincts, your reactions, and your need for comfort — you start moving the goalposts for yourself. You set new measurements. New expectations. New standards for who you are and what you're capable of.

Yet, you never arrive. There is no finish line. If you stop practicing, you stop progressing. But if you continue to work and keep reaching beyond the body, the growth becomes endless.

Einstein knew that, and to me, that's precisely what he meant when he said (and I repeat): *The true value of a human being is determined primarily by how he has attained liberation from the self.*

To be spiritual is to be authentic

The list that follows — The Plays — will guide you toward the spiritual behaviors. These are the habits, the mindsets, and the practices that reflect Omega-level awareness. But before we dive in, remember this: To be spiritual is to be authentic. Not the curated, polished version of yourself, not the one attached to roles or masks, but the real you. This is you without anything body-based attached.

The more often you act in alignment with that self, the one not driven by fear, validation, lust, or control the more spiritual you become. Every time you act with choice instead of urge — every time you override biology in favor of wisdom — you climb the scale of spiritual maturity. The more you can discern between what is biological and what is spiritual, the more clearly you will see the path forward, and the higher you'll rise in your evolution.

Why this is difficult even when we want it

It's important to pause here and acknowledge something deeper — this work is hard, even when you want it. Especially when you want it.

Like pushing through the final mile of a long run or hitting that last rep on your hundredth pushup, spiritual growth requires you to fight against the very biological system, no matter what feedback — whether fear, stress, anxiety, jealousy, or self-esteem — is trying to get you to do something that isn't actually in your best interest.

Your body doesn't want growth. It wants comfort. It wants the familiar. It wants safety because safety means survival. If you do choose to walk the Omega path, you must practice beating your own biology. Not once. Not occasionally. But consistently.

You must outwit your programming. You must override the urges that want you to be small, safe, and stuck. Every time you push past fatigue, your body pushes back harder. And it doesn't just push back with muscle pain. It does it with myopic biological urges, followed by self-talk carefully crafted to sound like wisdom.

"Maybe this isn't the right time."

"You're pushing too hard."

"Let's try again tomorrow."

"This isn't worth it."

That voice is not your intuition. Your automated defense mechanism — your body's last-ditch effort — keeps you small, predictable, and safe. But then something else kicks in. A voice beyond the body. A spiritual interjection. And it says:

"Go."

"Now."

"You choose."

That's the moment of override. Every great athlete, every great leader, and every man or woman who's ever become something more has learned to linger in that space. They learned to stand a little longer than their body wanted. To move forward even when everything said to stop.

The truth is, the whole system is stacked against you.

That spiritual voice — the one telling you to keep going — doesn't have a dedicated hormone to back it up. It doesn't flood your system with adrenaline. It doesn't get help from cortisol or glucose.

At best, it's rewarded with endorphins or dopamine — *but only after* you've committed. Only after you've chosen to suffer first. Yes, it's rigged. It's rigged to make you fold.

It's not just biology — the whole world is geared to make you quit. Very few people will understand why you're pushing when it's easier to sit. Very few people go beyond. Even fewer stay there.

Paradox is the path

Almost all spiritual work is a paradox. You'll be asked to fight against what your body and mind say they want. You'll be asked to let go in the very moment your ambition screams to hold on. You'll be called to act with restraint when your ego tells you to dominate. You'll need to have *faith* instead of *control*.

And you'll find dozens more paradoxes like these on your path, especially when you're fighting the urge to stop and every signal in your mind and body is telling you to quit. A deeper part of you knows *this is precisely when it matters most*.

Follow, don't achieve

This next section and the practices that follow aren't something to accomplish. They're something to follow. This is not a finish line. It's a fluid process. The goal isn't perfection. It's presence. Your only job is to stay in the game. To keep practicing. Everything else will follow.

From archetype to authenticity

With the understanding and motivation built in Part I — how men are in trouble, how our programming runs deep, how our upbringing and society try to define us — and with tools gained in Part II — awareness, vulnerability, presence — we arrive at this question:

What now? How do we behave?

The following chart shows how certain traits have traditionally been defined under Alpha and Sigma archetypes, and how they transform under the Omega mindset.

The Omega defies labels. He is not an archetype.

These comparisons can help you map your own progress. And remember this: no matter where you fall on the scale, you can leap directly into the Omega behaviors. You can shed every mask and skip the performance. The Omega isn't an identity. It's a decision.

Trait	Alpha	Sigma	Omega (You)
Motivation	Power, Control	Freedom, Independence	Purpose, Inner Truth
Confidence	Loud, Dominant	Silent, Detached	Quiet, Rooted, Unshakable
Validation	External (status, success, approval)	Self-Contained (no need for others)	Internal (spiritual grounding, self-respect)
Relationships	Dominate, Lead	Avoid, Lone Wolf	Deeply Connect, Elevate Others
Drive	Compete to Win	Compete with Self	Grow to Serve Purpose
Strength	Physical, Assertive	Mental, Autonomous	Spiritual, Disciplined, Resilient
Legacy	Status & Success	Autonomy	Impact, Authentic Legacy

The Playbook (i.e., the spiritual behaviors)

The traits in the table are not ones you're born with; they are practiced, repeated, and refined. They're the spiritual behaviors that define the Omega. They're not achievements but choices made again and again until they become your nature.

Before we get into The Plays, a question may arise: How does being an Omega help me? How does it help one at work? Or with relationships? Have you asked that question? While we will go into deeper detail about that in the closing chapter, let me give you a few of the high points motivating you to connect to The Playbook and Plays below.

To begin with, the first monumental reason is to STOP the downward trend of men. To be a real man. To declare freedom from all masculinity archetypes so you can stand alone. To stand free, powerful, strong, and invincible, while also being humble, vulnerable, kind, giving, gracious, compassionate, loving, and authentic. All those traits also create the most powerful, yet subtle forces that control all things: energy. No one has explained this better than Dr. David Hawkins in his trilogy, starting with *Power vs. Force*.

Spiritual behavior radiates power. Power is derived from the energetic signature of consciousness an Omega carries — it calms rooms, heals patterns, and shifts legacies. This type of energy is both masculine and feminine; it sees, incorporates, and manages many things, not just the self.

Once you've read The Plays, ask yourself to imagine what relationships — romantic relationships — work. Or you may focus on what anything else would be like if you implemented these fifteen Plays below.

Play 1: Omegas Do Not Fear Death

Let's begin with the hardest one first.

Remember, this is a practice, so allow me to frame it that way from the start.

The Omega is always working toward deeper awareness. He is constantly refining his ability to discern what comes from the body (*Stop, we are tired*) and what arises from the spirit (*Tired is good, keep going*).

An Omega knows that every biological urge is rooted in one thing: the body's drive not to die. The body's mission is survival. Not expansion. Not evolution.

Just don't die today.

But the goal of the Omega isn't to avoid death; it's to live fully. In fact, if one is not choosing to live and live well, then they are missing the very purpose of life: to live! That's what it means to be spiritual. Not reckless, not hedonistic, but aligned with something beyond fear—even beyond the fear of dying.

In the Plays that follow, you'll see why this doesn't lead to indulgence. But we must start here because fear of death drives so many reactive, impulsive, self-sabotaging behaviors. Fear of death makes men shrink. Fear of death makes men chase control. Fear of death makes men betray themselves in the name of staying "safe". Fear of death causes men to choose masks they think will lead them beyond death at that moment. Yet none of this is masculine, or even behaving or acting with strength.

The Omega looks death in the face and remains calm.

Remember, the body's fear shows up not just in life-or-death moments but in everyday discomfort, tiredness, hesitation, and worry. These are all shadows of the same biological script trying to keep you safe, not free.

The question is, do you know what being afraid of dying means?

Can you pull in that awareness to contextualize? Keep in mind that tired muscles signaling the brain, and the brain saying, "stop running!" is a response to save your life, and so is anxiety, depression, stress, fear, worry, doubt, and a host of other emotions.

The Omega looks the fear of death in the face, not because he wants to die, but because he knows that how and when we die is mostly not up to us. And, if it's not up to us, what's the point of anxiety, fear, or wasted energy? The Omega understands that the thing to fear is not death, but a life spent trying to prevent it.

"In avoiding death, many men unintentionally avoid life."

Let me give you a real-life example. Not long ago, I was flying overseas. The plane hit turbulence — rough, unpredictable, and the kind that jerks you awake. My mom, who was flying with me, was scared. She shared how much she hated the turbulence. You could hear the anxiety in her voice. The fear of dying had surfaced in this discussion, and it was loud. Automatic. Unfiltered.

My response to the same turbulence?

Peace.

I said to myself: "there's nothing I can do. If this plane goes down, it goes down. I'll be grateful for the time I've had on Earth. I'll count my blessings. I'll engage death humbly because it's not in my hands."

I wasn't faking it. I wasn't being stoic for show. I felt calm, clarity, and gratitude. This is what it means to not fear death.

How this shows up daily

Beyond flights and turbulence, how does this look in real life? It's how we respond when we get tired during a workout. The body says, "you might die. Slow down." The Omega says: "thanks for your input. I'll decide when I stop."

It's in how we treat women. We chase to procreate. We build illusions of "love" or "need" rooted in the primal urge to pass on genes. We tell ourselves stories. Underneath, though, it's biological.

It's in how we eat. We chase comfort foods because we feel safe, and fasting is good for us physically and spiritually. But it's hard. Why? Because the body doesn't like hard. The body sees "hard" as a threat. The body associates "hard" with potential death. But doing hard things is how we grow. And spiritual growth comes from doing the hard thing on purpose.

Easy equals safety. Hard equals expansion. The myopic mind and fragile ego don't like expansion; they like survival. But the Omega knows that growth lives in discomfort — and that death will come either way.

Omega reminder:

Your body fears death every day, not just when danger is obvious but even when you're tired, worried, or doubting yourself. Remember: fear is biological; the choice is spiritual.

Next challenge:

Today, catch one moment where your body says, "Stop," "Slow down," or "You might fail." Pause. Smile. Choose to act anyway, even if it's just for one extra pushup, one extra minute, one extra breath.

Reflection:

Tonight, ask yourself: *Where today did I recognize fear for what it truly was—just biology, not reality?*

Write it down, even if it was a small moment. Awareness turns fear into fuel.

Play 2: Live with Funeral Wisdom, i.e. Humility

This play builds on the one above, but with a nuance.

It's about remembering what matters. Think of the clarity that comes at a funeral. Petty concerns fall away. Egos dissolve. The noise gets quiet. You reflect on life, not drama. To live with humility means to live as if you've just come from a funeral, carrying the kind of wisdom we often forget when we're back in traffic, back in arguments, back in life. This is how the Omega practices emotional discipline in the face of what I call SLS: Stupid Little Shit.

Road rage. Getting cut off. Needing to be right. Pointless arguments. Holding back the truth because "it might not go over well." Replaying what you should have said in a conversation. All of this is SLS. And we engage with it constantly. Sometimes, even holding back the truth out of fear of disapproval is another form of SLS prioritizing image over integrity. But an Omega sees it for what it is: noise from the body, fueled by the ego. And he practices not engaging.

Just like running, the body always interjects. Always. Feel this. Say that. React now.

But just as the Omega practices pushing past fatigue in a workout, he also practices pushing past the urge to react to nonsense. He chooses — because the Omega always chooses.

Omega reminder:

Humility isn't weakness; it's wisdom born from the truth that most of what angers us simply does not matter.

Next challenge:

Today, when something petty provokes you — a rude driver, a slight at work — pause and internally say: *"SLS: Stupid Little Shit." Then smile and let it go.*

Reflection:

Tonight, ask yourself: *Where today did I choose peace over pettiness?* Honor even one small moment of restraint.

Play 3: Omegas Do Not Complain

This one might sound simple, but it's not. It's deceptively powerful.

To complain is to act superior. It's the body's sneaky way of restoring a sense of control. It says: "this shouldn't be happening to me." It says, "i'm better than this."

Complaining isn't the same as advocating for yourself. It's not the same as expressing a need, setting a boundary, or stating an opinion.

Complaining is emotional theater. It soothes the ego and performs righteousness for the imaginary audience in our minds. Deep down, the Omega knows that all experiences are neutral.

All things are equal, and, perhaps most importantly, the Omega doesn't need to tell anyone anything self-serving. Every time we complain, we leak spiritual energy. Every time we stay silent and centered, we strengthen it.

This brings us perfectly to the next behavior.

Omega reminder:

Complaining feeds the ego, not the spirit. Silence, when chosen consciously, feeds your inner strength.

Next challenge:

Catch yourself mid-complaint, even if just in thought. Replace it with: *"this is neutral. I choose how I respond."*

Reflection:

Tonight, ask yourself: *Did I notice when my mind wanted to complain today?* What changed when I didn't give it my energy?

Play 4: Omegas Do Not Need External Validation

This one goes deeper than you think. To say an Omega doesn't need external validation isn't just about ignoring praise or brushing off criticism; it's about neutralizing their meaning altogether.

To an Omega, insults and compliments are the same. They're just words. Projections. Reflections of someone else's programming, perspective, or positionality.

Whether someone praises us or attacks us doesn't define us. Their words are not the truth. They're perceptions. And yes, those perceptions may hold information, but the information does not need to contain any emotion. Information is neutral. It doesn't require that we feel good because someone likes us or feel hurt because someone doesn't.

Compliments are not "good". Insults are not "bad." They're mirrors, or fragments of another person's lens. The Omega listens if there's something to learn. But he doesn't feed on it. He doesn't need it to feel strong, whole, or worthy. This detachment is what gives the Omega power, not power over others, but power over himself.

Omega reminder:

No opinion about you, good or bad, can add or subtract from who you truly are.

Next challenge:

Today, when you receive either a compliment or criticism, pause internally and say: *"this is information, not identity."*

Reflection:

Tonight, ask yourself: *How did it feel to stay centered when others tried to define me today?*

Play 5: Omegas Understand Power Is Not Force

The Omega does not chase power for the sake of being powerful.

Instead, he understands this: To have true power is to live from authenticity.

And when your authenticity is truly aligned with your deepest values, you don't need to assert anything. You simply are.

This is what Einstein was pointing to. The value of a man is not in what he achieves but in how far he's freed himself from the ego-driven self.

And that means understanding the difference between biological energy and spiritual energy.

Biological energy says:

- "Stop. This is hard."
- "You're tired."
- "You need to preserve."

Spiritual energy says:

- "Keep going."
- "You choose this."
- "You are more than your fatigue."

Here's the nuance: biological energy feels louder because it's physical. Because it comes with chemicals like cortisol, adrenaline, or fear.

Spiritual energy is softer. It doesn't come with a rush. It doesn't shout. But it's more sustainable. More resilient. More true.

Real example: the fatigue voice in training

When we're out of shape, the self-talk that tells us to quit shows up early: "you're already tired" or "you're not strong enough."

But the longer we train, the later that voice shows up. We override it more easily. It moves further into the background. You don't overcome the biological voice by fighting it. You overcome it by recognizing it earlier each time and choosing anyway. That's how we know: the voice is biological. And it's not reliable.

But spiritual override is different. Once you've defied the body, even once you remember, you know you can. You've accessed that gear before, and now it's available to you again. That's not conditioning, it's awareness.

Unlike physical endurance, spiritual resilience doesn't erode when you stop. You don't "lose" it, you just choose not to engage it. But once you've overridden biology, you've proven something deeper to yourself. Let this principle expand. Don't limit it to exercise. Use it in conversations. In parenting. In work. In relationships. Let the spirit take over everywhere.

Omega reminder:

True power is quiet. It radiates without needing to convince, chase, or prove.

Next challenge:

Today, in one moment where you feel the urge to "push", stop. Instead, stand in your truth without forcing anything.

Reflection:

Tonight, ask yourself: *Where today did I allow power to flow without needing force?* Even once is enough to grow.

Play 6: Omegas Have Reverence for Life

This one is a paradox, but by now, you're used to those. We've already said that Omegas don't fear death; now we must say something that appears the opposite: Omegas have deep reverence for life.

To live without fear of dying doesn't mean we live carelessly; it means we live consciously with a deep appreciation for the preciousness of existence. True mastery is not detachment from life; it's devotion to it. The Omega values the *impermanence* of all things. From that awareness, he shows care. He shows discipline. He shows restraint.

He does not take what he doesn't need. He does not consume in excess. He does not harm for convenience. He honors the sacredness of being alive by honoring the life around him.

That includes how we eat. We don't need to kill unnecessarily, but we also don't fear eating what has been provided. We act with mindfulness — not shame, and not indulgence.

This reverence puts a cap on gluttony. On greed. On waste. It reminds us that to fear death is to hoard, but to respect life is to share. To give. To take only what's needed and leave the rest behind with gratitude. Restraint is not a limitation; restraint is reverence in action.

Omega reminder:

To live without fearing death is noble. To live honoring life is divine.

Next challenge:

Today, practice reverence: waste less, appreciate more. Before your next meal or moment of beauty, silently say: *"thank you."*

Reflection:

Tonight, ask yourself: *Where today did I honor life by appreciating it rather than consuming it unconsciously?*

Play 7: Omegas Do Not Compete

Let's be clear: competition exists. People will compete with you. But — the Omega doesn't take the bait. Why? Because he knows that competition implies scarcity. It says: "there's not enough." It says: "if I don't win, I lose." It says: "I need this to matter."

The Omega doesn't play that game.

He shows up. He gives his best. He's not attached to outcomes; he's devoted to the process. He trains for strength, not trophies. He creates for love, not likes. He speaks the truth, not applause. And that is deeply spiritual.

Animals compete for territory, for dominance, and for mates. They hoard. They chase. They can't see past the next nut. Humans do the same when they live biologically. More followers. More deals. More square footage. More validation.

But the Omega? He sees the forest. He lives in alignment, not pursuit. He knows his principles are what yield bounty, not his striving. Winning for the Omega is not about defeating others. It's about defeating limitations within himself. When you live up to your values, your success becomes inevitable, not because you chased it but because you attracted it.

Omega reminder:

The Omega's only competition is with who he was yesterday.

Next challenge:

Today, notice one moment where comparison creeps in.

Smile. Refocus inward. Ask yourself: *"am I better aligned with my values today than yesterday?"*

Reflection:

Tonight, ask yourself: *Where today did I choose process over proving?*

Play 8: Omegas Give without Gain

Omegas care deeply. But their caring is free of strings, no need for gratitude, control, or validation. If we give, it's because we choose to, not because we need anything in return. True giving isn't leverage or scorekeeping.

For an Omega, giving is a way of life. It is not to impress, validate, or control. When one has everything and needs nothing, giving becomes effortless. And giving without gain raises our vibration, our spirit, and our power — or as Hawkins would say, "not force".

"The moment you give to get, you didn't give at all." – Omega Code

"For it is in giving that we receive." – St. Francis of Assisi

Play 8 hits home for me. For decades, I gave my time, my words, and even my values. But — I gave them with the hidden goal of being liked or accepted. It drained me, because what I wanted in return rarely came to fruition. And when it inevitably didn't, I felt resentful, even ashamed. Those were low-percentage shots in the dark; acts of giving for gain that cost me more than they gave. Only when I let go of needing anything back did giving finally become real and freeing.

Omega reminder:

True compassion needs nothing in return; it is the act of giving without invisible contracts.

Next challenge:

Today, offer one act of kindness, a compliment, a favor, or a thank you, expecting absolutely nothing back.

Reflection:

Tonight, ask yourself: *Where today did I give freely without needing acknowledgment?*

Play 9: Omegas: "No Identity Needed"

As an Omega, we know we use the term as a guide, not an identity. As ones that do not need validation, we also don't need identity. How often do you see, or have you heard other men declare they are an "Alpha Male" or take pride in sharing that unilaterally self-declared archetype? Their Alphaness on display? Why would anyone confident or internally strong need to express that? They need it because they need validation. That validation is back to one seeking biological superiority on the Darwinian scale; true or just projection does not matter. As humans, the perception of something has been proven to trick many people.

To be an Omega is to go beyond biology, so anything that smells or acts like an animal is to be practiced out of, including presenting falsehoods or making statements that do not need to be said.

Omega reminder:

Identity is a tool, not a trophy. True freedom requires no badge.

Next challenge:

Today, resist any urge to label yourself or prove yourself. Live your values quietly and let your actions speak.

Reflection:

Tonight, ask yourself: *Where today did I simply live my truth without needing anyone to notice?*

Play 10: Omegas Avoid Argument, and They Don't Defend

Before we go into this play further, do you know the definition of "arguing"?

For this book, the definition is, "arguing is attempting to change another person's mind about something." Defending oneself is the same thing with the script flipped. For this play, arguing simply means trying to change someone else's mind, and defending means trying to convince someone of your own worth. So why is it an Omega play?

To begin with, Omegas focus on what is in their control rather than things that are not. Presenting a persuasive position when sharing one's own views is not an argument. Working to actively care or have a need to change anyone's mind about anything is an effort towards control.

Omegas have no reason to control anyone, nor, needless to say, the minds of others. Magic can truly happen when one does not argue or defend. We can actively talk, listen, share ideas, and be open-minded toward understanding other views.

The next step, when embattled with the possibility of an argument, is to find a solution to varied opinions, not to argue or defend. Resolution-oriented versus conflict-oriented. An Omega knows the donkey and the tiger story all too well and strives not to be the donkey or, as the story goes, the tiger.

Omega reminder:

Needing to win an argument is needing to control. The Omega seeks understanding, not dominance.

Next challenge:

Today, if a disagreement arises, practice deep listening without needing to correct or defend.

Just witness.

Reflection:

Tonight, ask yourself: *Where today did I choose peace over persuasion?*

Play 11: Omegas Know Being Alive is Purpose

An Omega doesn't chase a grand mission to prove worth. An Omega also knows that purpose isn't a vocation or a way to earn money. Purpose is a state of being and understanding that being alive is the highest purpose one can serve. Just ask Viktor Frankl.

You don't exist to win at life; you exist to live it. There's a difference between living life and preventing death. An Omega knows that every second he is alive, he has the opportunity to improve. That can only occur by connecting to the Play: Omegas live with the purpose of life and nothing else.

To embody this Play allows the embodiment of so many others, like Reverence for Life and the idea that Omegas do not need external validation.

Omega reminder:

Your highest purpose isn't a title or achievement; it's the courage to live fully, moment to moment.

Next challenge:

Today, notice one small moment where you forget you "need" to accomplish anything and simply enjoy being alive.

Reflection:

Tonight, ask yourself: Where today did I embody living itself as my highest purpose?

Even noticing one moment is mastery.

Play 12: "I Choose"

Ultimately, to be authentic or spiritual — to act with spiritual behaviors — is to choose how to act. Choice means power over reactive behavior. It means acting beyond the impulses of what Nietzsche called "the beast".

No one proved this more than Viktor Frankl, who wrote of the space between stimulus and response. That small space is where freedom lives. We must all learn to pause in that moment and decide how to act, what we want to believe, and who we choose to be — or not to be, i.e., to avoid wearing another mask.

An Omega is never a puppet of his environment. He doesn't blame triggers, moods, stresses, or wounds for how he acts. He chooses with his own compass, not ruled by emotional tugs at the unhealed aspects of his psyche.

- He can feel anger, but he chooses patience.

- He can feel fear, but he chooses courage.

- He can feel doubt, but he chooses presence.

Omega behavior isn't about feeling like it. It's about choosing alignment, even when biology begs otherwise. This too is a practice, and a Play the Omega works toward. That's what makes it spiritual.

The Omega owns his actions the way a master craftsman owns his tools and his craft: patiently, consistently, and intentionally. By choosing this way, he lives with power over biology and with trust in something deeper: intuition, faith, and spirit.

Omega reminder:

True freedom is not controlling life; it's controlling your response to life.

Next challenge:

Today, find one moment where your emotions pull hard and choose your action consciously rather than reacting automatically.

Reflection:

Tonight, ask yourself: *Where today did I choose my behavior, even when it was hard?*

That choice is your highest strength.

Play 13: Omegas Practice Daily

Living as an Omega isn't a title you earn and frame on the wall. It's a practice you renew every day. You practice choosing wisdom over impulse. You practice listening beyond the noise. You practice strength through gentleness and power through restraint.

Some days, you'll feel aligned. On other days, you'll stumble. It doesn't matter. What matters is that you try.

The Omega knows: "Practice doesn't make perfect. Practice is Dharma." The effort is the path. Not the image. Not the applause. Not even the outcome. Only the commitment to try and practice daily.

To me, and from my research and understanding, now, Dharma means being on a path of always trying to live in the right action without attachment to results, as the Bhagavad Gita professes.

Omega reminder:

You are not a finished product; you are a living practice.

Next challenge:

Today, dedicate just 60 seconds to intentional Omega behavior, whether through patience, courage, humility, or restraint.

Reflection:

Tonight, ask yourself: *Where today did I practice being an Omega, even imperfectly?* The attempt itself is sacred.

Play 14: Omegas Steer Self-talk

Not every thought that floats into your head deserves an audience. An Omega knows that many thoughts are derived from the voice of programming, the impact of past trauma, the wins, the losses, the lessons—but not the choice.

While Play 12 asks the Omega to choose, Play 14 asks us to steer before we choose. Essentially, Play 14 is what to do with that "small moment in time before stimulus and response".

Most of what your mind mutters during the day is noise: old programming, overhyped fears, and borrowed beliefs. Yet the mind is also an amazing tool, one with insights, experience, ideas, and the power of contemplation, as well as sabotage, dissent, and chaos. The mind deserves to be listened to, but only in places where we steer its gaze.

Michael Singer captures it simply in *The Untethered Soul*:

> *There is nothing more important to true growth than realizing that you are not the voice of the mind—you are the one who hears it.*

The Omega learns to ignore noise, not by fighting it, but by steering around it. Most importantly, he learns to acknowledge, with awareness, whether the voices have value and bountiful or blather.

The Omega assesses — rather than suppresses — this inner dialogue. He's not afraid of how these voices make him feel. Instead, he allows them in and uses awareness, vulnerability, and the goal of authenticity to shed light on the value of this self-talk.

The Omega works toward avoiding internal arguments; he doesn't wrestle with every insecurity. He doesn't validate every complaint. Instead, he listens selectively, like tuning a radio. He asks: "is this voice survival?" or "is this voice spirit?"

Marcus Aurelius once said: "you have power over your mind—not outside events. Realize this, and you will find strength." The Omega embodies this strength by learning to steer his thoughts moment to moment, by the compass of intention, not by the weather of passing thoughts.

Omega reminder:

Not every thought deserves your attention. Wisdom is choosing which plant to water.

Next challenge:

Today, when negative or anxious thoughts arise, pause and ask: *"Is this voice survival or spirit?"* Listen, then steer.

Reflection:

Tonight, ask yourself: *Where today did I steer my mind rather than letting it steer me?* Awareness is mastery.

Play 15: Omegas Meditate

The Omega does not treat stillness as a luxury. He treats it as fuel. He recognizes that there is power in peacefulness. He does not waste it but seeks it intentionally. Meditation, whether sitting silently, walking mindfully, or breathing with awareness, is not an escape from life. It is practice.

Meditation is a practice of learning how to manage thoughts in a controlled, dedicated setting so that, day-to-day, our ability to follow Play 14 becomes automatic, even subconscious.

Every day, the world floods your senses with noise, urgency, and competition. Meditation is where you return to your own field. To your own center. To the place where power renews, and fear dissolves.

The Omega doesn't meditate to become someone else. He meditates to remember who he already is underneath the noise. Still. Grounded. Unshakable.

Omega reminder:

Stillness isn't weakness; it's where your deepest power lives.

Next challenge:

Today, spend five minutes, even if it's just breathing quietly, reconnecting to your own field of strength.

Reflection:

Tonight, ask yourself: *How did it feel to return to my center today, even briefly?* Every return builds resilience.

Comments From Brad Kearns

"You can leap directly into Omega behaviors, no matter where you're starting from." Rejoice! It's urgent that we start appreciating how success looks different for everyone. This is in stark contrast to the alpha-dominated world ruled by the biggest, strongest, loudest, most aggressive, and most athletic.

The book Season of Life by Jeffrey Marx, profiling the love-based coaching style of former NFL player Joe Ehrmann, had a good take on it. The book explains how men are socialized to measure their self-worth in three ways: athletic ability, economic success, and sexual conquest. Ehrmann calls these the "false masculinity" standards - shallow and destructive ideals that lead men away from emotional honesty, empathy, and true connection.

Sounds incredibly simple, superficial, and reductionist, but I wonder if anyone reading can strongly counter this premise? As a high school football coach,

Ehrmann teaches what he calls "true masculinity", based on building strong, loving relationships, living with purpose, and serving others.

Today is the day for the shy, quiet, diminutive, non-athletic, non-competitive types to rise up and be the best they can be - in the realm of being connected, spiritual, grounded, resilient and the other good stuff in the Omega column. We no longer have to trudge through life with a giant scoreboard shining down on us, showing loss after loss to those better equipped to prevail in the false masculinity categories.

Embracing more evolved and fulfilling possibilities reminds me of the hilarious and brilliant lyrics from the rapper Richie Rich, guesting in the Tupac song "Ratha Be Ya Ni**a":

♦

"You can ride out with sport coat, to get your lobster and crab
Cause all I got is conversation and a gang of stab
And I'm a listen when it hurts, I'm a hang out but never stay
Smoke blunts but leave them stunts to Super Dave
I'll be your ni**a, as long as we can understand
That I's the ni**a and sport coat can be the man
He wine and dine, but me and you we whine and grind
And when he on the field I keep you on the sidelines"

In case you're a little unclear with some of the raunchy nuance, ChatGPT helps us out with this brilliant poetic analysis:

The speaker is drawing a contrast between himself and a more conventional, wealthy man who tries to impress a woman with money and fine dining ("lobster and crab"). The rapper, by contrast, doesn't offer luxury — just real talk, street credibility, and physical intimacy ("conversation and a gang of stab").

He's saying:

- He's genuine and emotionally present ("I'm a listen when it hurts"),
- But he keeps things casual ("hang out but never stay"),
- He's not flashy ("leave them stunts up to Super Dave"),
- And while another man might try to court her respectfully ("he winin' and dinin'"), the rapper and the woman share a raw, physical, unfiltered connection ("we wine and grind").

The line "keep him on the sidelines" means while the other man plays the role of a polite suitor, the rapper is the one she's really with — the one "on the field." In essence: He's portraying himself as the real but rough alternative to the polished man — offering authenticity, attitude, and intimacy instead of money or pretense."

Well, what are you waiting for? With sufficient guidance from Dave, and further inspiration from Mr. Ehrmann and Mr. Rich, let's go out there and be ourselves and be comfortable with that - once and for all.

Closing Chapter 11

Wow! That was a lot. Great job, and congratulations. You made it this far.

Chapter 11 can be heavy, and you've already begun the work by reaching this point. If it feels difficult or even overwhelming sometimes, remember this: Difficulty is proof that you're standing at the edge of old limits. However, we must also respect this truth: New ways of thinking, new perspectives, and new choices often involve fear, and they take energy and brainpower.

That's natural. It's part of the process. The goal is to embody the Omega path so that you use less brainpower and less emotional friction for the rest of your life. And you're already choosing to move beyond the old ways. You don't have to do it perfectly. You only have to keep choosing.

This isn't about force. It's about trust. It's about remembering that the Omega path isn't a finish line. It's a way of being.

And you're already on it.

Warmup for Chapter 12

In the next chapter, we'll dive into how to sustain this new way of living — not through more force, but through stillness connection and a deeper spiritual resilience.

You'll learn how simple practices like meditation, reflection, and daily intentionality can build the kind of spiritual core that nothing — not fear, not stress, not loss — can shake.

Because being an Omega isn't just about awakening.

It's about staying awake.

Chapter 12:

The Challenges & The Spiritual Strength of the Omega Code

You might feel confused right now.

If you're like many who reach this point on the path, a few questions will have started to bubble up. From my personal experience, from countless conversations with others, and from years of research, I've found that most people eventually arrive at something like the following:

- How do I live this way?

- Why does everything feel so contradictory?

- Why does this path seem to go against everything society praises as success, especially for a man?

But beneath all those questions, I think the real questions — the ones most people hesitate to ask out loud — are these:

- Why would someone even choose this path?

- Is it actually better?

- Will it help me?

Standing now on the other side of those questions, on the Omega side, I can say yes to the latter two questions without hesitation. Yes, it is better and will help you, but what does "better" mean? Let's define it first.

Better feels easier. More fluid. Fewer obstacles. Fewer tragedies. Better looks like more of the things that bring joy, but come with less effort.

However, that answer comes with a caveat, because the truth is that this path shouldn't be taken for gain.

The Omega path isn't about performance, status, or ego. It isn't a tactic for happiness, validation, or to "get the girl." It's for something more profound: internal truth. Alignment. A life lived in support of higher ideals. And in that alignment, the truly "better life" arrives.

Yet, here's the paradox — I didn't start this journey from some selfless motive; I started it to improve my life. Maybe you did, too. Perhaps you're here because the old ways stopped functioning, and you're hoping this one will finally work.

Here's what I discovered: the "better" comes in waves. Waves that meet what Einstein once said about the true value of a human being. At first, better shows up as personal gain. But as you change, the intention changes, and the meaning of "better" changes with it. As personal gain sheds, true gain begins to flow back to you. That's where most of us begin.

This is one of the central paradoxes of the spiritual path. You begin it to get something. The further you go, the more you realize the only way to truly receive is to let go of wanting what you started with in the first place.

So, let's return to the first question: Would you choose this path?

For me, the answer is still yes. Absolutely. Unshakably.

Or as Carl Jung put it, *"the privilege of a lifetime is to become who you truly are"*

But that answer must become yours. It can not be inherited from me or anyone else. Rumi once wrote: *When you know your why, any how is possible.* I'm not saying it's easy, though. There are challenges — but these challenges will help you uncover that "why" and discover what waits for you on the other side.

Let's take a look at those challenges.

Challenge #1 – Doubt

To begin with, this path is not the easy way. Men have been taking the easy way for decades, and look where it has gotten them. The easy way is to look at the latest and greatest public figure — John Wayne or Drake — and try to emulate them. But — here's the thing — if we emulate the man of the day, we're destined not to be our own selves. Still, it's the easy way out because it's easier to emulate or copy others and far more challenging to be an original.

This is a paradox in and of itself: men choose to emulate someone who found success by being original. They then think that copying them (the original) will make them an original, too.

Yeah, not so.

As the ad once said, "Nothing like the real thing, baby!" Unfortunately, most of us never put practice into place to become the real thing. It's easier and more natural for the human-animal side of us to take shortcuts and copy. It's biological. It's instinctual.

Think back to the animal. Resting and having things be easy is "Darwinian Survivability". The easy way is ingrained in our DNA: to conserve energy and avoid pushing too hard. But growth comes from pushing beyond easy. That's not just a motivational phrase; it's a biological truth. It's science. The human brain is wired to resist change. It's called a "threat response". When we consider doing something new, even something that might help us, our amygdala reacts as if we're under attack. The heart rate rises. Cortisol floods the body. And suddenly, the easiest option is to stay the same. The body and mind collude to keep you where you are.

Here are four ways that resistance shows up.

1. Fatigue: You feel tired when it's time to change. The body says, "Not today."

2. Rationalization: You create smart-sounding reasons why this path isn't right for you or not right now.

3. Avoidance: You stay busy with other things. You check your phone. You scroll. You do "productive" tasks that let you avoid the real work.

4. Doubt: You question whether change is even necessary. You convince yourself that your current situation isn't that bad.

We like to think we're logical, but most resistance to growth isn't rational — it's biological. The mind rationalizes. It invents excuses. It justifies staying the same.

Choosing a new path requires not just open-mindedness but open-heartedness. It's not just about thinking differently. It's about feeling differently. It's about acting beyond survival instincts and trusting something higher than biology.

Challenge #2 – The Body

We are biological machines wired for survival, attraction, reproduction, and social bonding. Most people, without even realizing it, are ruled entirely by that wiring.

We crave procreation in the form of sex. We crave food. We crave love in the form of acceptance and validation. We crave belonging.

These are not abstract desires; they are primal urges. Ancient instincts. Hard-coded scripts from a time when not belonging meant death. But here's the problem: those biological programs haven't been updated, even though our psyche and world have. We no longer live in tribal caves where being accepted by the group meant the difference between life and death; it's just that our bodies haven't gotten the memo.

The body says:

- chase validation
- earn approval
- don't get rejected
- postulate for the sex

And do all of this to win the girl, and be admired. It appears to be the "survival of the fittest".

We chase a fleeting feeling of connection or chase someone who makes us feel seen. Even if it costs you your values. Even if it makes you lie, cheat, perform, or betray your deeper truth. Even if you sabotage your own life, relationships, and self-worth.

But what if that feeling of being seen didn't need to be earned? What if you had already been seen? What if you were already loved?

After Dave passed, I did a guided ayahuasca ceremony. During this ceremony, Dave spoke to me. He said something I'll never forget:

> *If people knew how loved they were, they'd stop doing so many stupid things to feel it.*

That hit me hard because it's true. That sentence cracked my thinking and heart wide open. It named what I hadn't admitted: our deepest pain isn't from reality but from perception. We think we're unloved. We do desperate things to feel seen, but the truth is, we already are.

Years earlier, I stood at the edge of a second-story window, wondering if I should jump. I wasn't suicidal. I was biologically hijacked.

So much of our suffering, self-betrayal, and pain is not because we aren't loved; it's because we don't feel loved. This is based on thinking we are not longed for, at that moment. We don't feel it because we've outsourced that feeling to other people. People who are also scared, and who may be feeling broken or are likely to be chasing love in all the wrong places, just like I did, and maybe you.

This is the battleground. It's not a joust between good and evil, but between biology and truth.

The brain, in an effort to protect us, triggers a fear response when our identity is threatened. When we feel disconnected, uncertain, or excluded, the amygdala lights up like we're under physical attack. Even the idea of change can activate fight, flight, or freeze. And the body? It obeys. It numbs us. It exhausts us.

Standing at the edge of that second-story window, I was overwhelmed, broken inside, disconnected from everything that once gave me identity. My nervous system was screaming for relief. My mind was looking for an escape hatch.

It wasn't some grand revelation that saved me; it was something quieter. The decision to pause. To not obey the urge. To sit in it. To not act from pain. That pause was the beginning of mastery. It was the first whisper of spiritual awareness. And I learned that the body protects, but the spirit guides.

The challenge is to learn to override biology. To rise above it. To become civilized, not in appearance but in essence. To stop letting the body run the show. Not to kill the body. Not to shame it. Not to repress it. But to parent it. To become the wise steward of your animal nature. To keep it at bay when it wants to take the wheel and crash the whole thing into a wall to feel a little attention or warmth.

To become enlightened, as I define it, is to be further along that path. Being able to keep your body in check so you can act from your highest wisdom instead of your lowest instinct. It's the hardest thing you'll ever do, but it's the only thing that will truly set you free.

Challenge #3 – Others

Most people will not understand your path. It is not common, and we live in a society where the majority assigns a higher perception of value. In truth, however, the majority means very little in this area.

Popularity doesn't equal truth. Mass agreement doesn't equal wisdom. IG or TikTok "likes" for a donut shop, movie, or burrito stand are one thing, but the way the majority live? That's another story.

Many of the most successful and impactful individuals on the planet meditate. (Not a majority, just a powerful few — Ray Dalio, Michael Phelps, LeBron James, Howard Stern, Jerry Seinfeld, Oprah Winfrey, etc.) Would you choose to be in the majority of humans who do NOT meditate, or the minority who have tried to keep this superpower practice secret?

For animals, majority means survival and safety in numbers. Don't get kicked out of the pack.

But what about breaking from the herd? That takes something: vulnerability, awareness, courage, and critical thinking.

It takes spiritual self-respect to look at the majority and say, "this is or isn't for me." Going against the majority (the herd or, as some put it, "sheeple") is to say, "just because everyone else lives this way, doesn't mean I should."

Here's what makes this challenge brutal — they will try to stop you. Not because they hate you, but because your freedom threatens them.

Your evolution becomes their mirror. If they're not ready to look at their own reflection, they'll try to shatter yours. When people can no longer control you, they'll try to control how others see you. They'll undermine you. They'll gossip. They'll label you. They'll frame your transformation as a failure or a phase. Why? Because your liberation exposes their captivity.

This resistance won't come from strangers; it will come from the ones you love most. Your parents. Siblings. Old best friends. Coaches. Teachers. Partners. The very people who once supported you will suddenly pull back or criticize your growth. This is what's called the "Crab Bucket Effect."

If you haven't heard of this effect, it comes from the behavior of crabs. If there is a group of crabs in a bucket and one tries to climb out, what do the others do? They pull it back in. If the crab persists, they may even break its legs — not out of hate but instinct. No crab can be allowed to escape if the rest believe escape is impossible.

Humans, in a sense, behave like crabs. Mediocrity has a loyalty clause. You become "the weird one", "the selfish one", "the arrogant one" in the minds of those around you. What you really are, though, is the one who got out.

In the realm of masculinity, most men are sheep. When they realize they're a Beta, they try to become an Alpha. All Betas are just Alphas in training. Once they've become Alpha and encounter a Sigma, they shift again. Now, all Alphas are Sigma-wannabes.

Each of these roles is based on the same outdated code: emulation, mimicry, mask-wearing. Each man chases what he believes will secure him a spot in the hierarchy of survival.

But the Omega doesn't climb that ladder. He burns it.

The Omega path is so rare — and that's why. It's also why it is so real. It's unconventional to put faith in a path you've never seen modeled. Most men know what it means to climb the masculine ladder to go from follower (Beta) to dominant (Alpha) to independent (Sigma). Few understand what it means to dismantle the whole thing.

The Omega path doesn't require more practice. It requires un-practicing. Letting go of everything you did to become a Beta, an Alpha, or a Sigma. The Omega lets go of the map entirely.

Sigma is often the confident Alpha, the one who trains in silence and studies masculinity to project cool control. But it's still a mask. The Omega wears no mask. He doesn't perform "intuition". He listens to it.

To be an Omega, you must follow a path that no one else around you is following. A path with no template. No external model. The path with no ladder to climb. The only thing to follow is your own spirit. A path that breaks away from Darwinian fear and embraces soul-level courage. A path that doesn't fear death because it has already faced it, inside.

As for me, when I question whether I've drifted off the path, I ask, "am I honoring my spirit deeply enough to walk this path today?"

To me, it feels like Viktor Frankl in Auschwitz, recalling how he and other prisoners hoped they were "worthy of their suffering." Worthy not by achievement but by dignity. Not by dominance but by depth. To live through hardship with honor. To meet life with the highest standards of being.

Challenge #4 — The Future as an Omega

What does it mean to be a man to you now?

Should it be defined?

Or should it be who you are without the programming?

Have you ever worn an Alpha mask — or any mask?

Maybe you were the type who adopted the "bad boy" image because it worked for your roommate in college. Or perhaps you didn't want to be invisible, so you wore what worked. But what if the real you was never invisible to begin with? Who were you before all that?

One quote that had a profound effect on me, and I say it to myself often, is by Eckhart Tolle:

> *The less of you you are, the more of you you will become.*

In other words, when you subtract the programming, your spirit finally shines. What all this means is that you need to stop thinking. Stop contemplating how to act, or who to be. The more you try to become "a man", the further you drift from being one. It's what Einstein meant when he said the true value of humans is in how much they become their Self.

I know this will create confusion. Yes, there are times when we do or must take on personas — namely when needed to uphold specific manners or standards in a certain setting. But understand that the moment needed for decorum is a state; it is not meant to be a trait. The goal is not to conform to life in all the little moments, but to carry our traits through life, only allowing states to interrupt our practice when dire and needed. To let our traits, our real practice and plans for being an Omega — the real us — solidify around our truth, not someone else's script.

And to be honest with you, that can make you feel lost. I've felt lost several times on this journey. Because when you stop wearing masks, the silence gets louder before it gets clearer.

The walk home

Joseph Campbell taught that the Hero's Journey, as exemplified in by Odysseus, does not end with the battle. The true ending is the return, the walk back to the village with the treasure of transformation. Nietzsche envisioned the Übermensch, rising above the herd to create his own values. Einstein reminded us that the worth of a man is measured by his liberation from the false self.

All of them pointed toward transcendence; breaking masks, slaying illusions, surpassing old scripts. But the Omega path adds something vital: what comes after the conquest. The walk home is not about carrying the prize of the sword but laying it down. It is the barefoot return, stripped of armor, where your life itself becomes the teaching.

This is the true heart of the Omega. To show strength through vulnerability. To embody everything this book has pointed to: authenticity, steadiness, practice, and presence. The Omega does not teach by force or command; he teaches by example. His quiet walk, lived in honesty and integrity, becomes the Ripple that others feel and follow.

1. The Daily Walk as an Omega

Now that he's transformed, how does he live?

This isn't about staying on a mountaintop, chanting mantras, and avoiding life. This is about coming down from the mountain with something tangible in your bones.

It's about showing up in the world not to win, not to prove, but to walk it rightly. To carry your peace into traffic, into conflict, into temptation, or into uncertainty. This is what it means to embody Omega energy in everyday life. There's a texture to it. The calm. The occasional hints of early loneliness. The groundedness that comes from no longer playing the peacock game.

You don't need others to tell you who you are. You've stopped renting your worth; now you own it. And even when the old voices show up — the ones that say you're not enough, not admired, not liked — you smile at them like old ghosts because stillness has taken their place. This stillness isn't passivity; it's presence. It's walking through life with your spiritual playbook — not in your head but in your muscle memory.

The Omega Man Roadmap

Here's what the journey looks like — not as theory, but as practice:

Stage	Description
Awareness	Recognize the script. See the Alpha/Survival Programming for what it is.
Be Vulnerable	Answer the call. Acknowledge the emptiness of old models.
Implement the Basics	Choose the Omega path. Reclaim spiritual, emotional, and relational sovereignty.
Daily Plays	Practice awareness, humility, emotional transmutation, and quiet power.
Behavior	The Return. Live authentically. Inspire others not by teaching, but by example.

Ask yourself:

- What does life feel like when you're no longer trying to win but to live rightly?

- What does it feel like to no longer chase validation but to embody worth?

This is the daily walk. It's the quiet strength. The unshakable rhythm of a man who became himself.

2. Integration: Bringing the Elixir Back

The Omega doesn't live in isolation. He doesn't ascend the mountain to stay there. He returns — changed — not louder, but deeper.

In his "Hero's Journey," Joseph Campbell called this moment The Return with the Elixir. He brings back the gift. The medicine. The truth is forged in fire from hard knocks. And that truth isn't a doctrine or a dogma; it's a way of being. It is what you now choose versus what you were once a slave to.

The Omega's elixir is emotional regulation. It's the spiritual behavior, presence, authenticity, spiritual steadiness, and conscious masculinity. He doesn't bring it to save others. He brings it because he can't live otherwise.

Here's what that looks like in real life:

The Omega shows the world and the ones closest to him that there is another form of masculinity. One that refuses to participate in locker-room bravado to earn approval. One that would never brag about "grabbing a woman's crotch" just to seem powerful. An Omega would never say he caught a 14-inch fish when it was really 13-and-a-half.

To be authentic is to be honest to a half-pound level. The Omega knows that honesty has more currency than boasting ever will. This is the gift others will feel. To stand tall without posturing. To be masculine without pretending to be "a real man". To embody a form of strength that is unthreatening, unforced, and completely unshakable.

It's not a soft masculinity. It's not a hard masculinity. It's something else entirely. It's the non-masculine masculine. The kind that doesn't need to prove it's a man at all.

This is the behavior we were meant to bestow, not the performative script that men have added to masculinity over the last 100 years. But a quiet truth. A living example. A better way.

But here's the tension: He returns to a world still in chaos. He walks through offices, relationships, and conversations that still run on ego and performance. And he must navigate that world while holding peace in his chest and truth in his spine.

People become confused when you no longer react the way the world expects. When you don't compete, provoke, perform, or posture, some will see you as weak. But the ones who are ready will feel it. They'll sense the frequency shift, and they'll lean in.

When one man changes, everyone around him is invited to evolve. Your son or daughter watches you choose presence over power. Your team learns that strength doesn't need to shout. Your partner feels seen, heard, and felt — not managed or seduced, but truly seen.

Even strangers may notice something in your tone, your timing, your quiet, and your presence. Albert Einstein once said:

> A human being is part of a whole called by us the 'universe,' a part limited in time and space. He experiences himself, his thoughts, and feelings as something separated from the rest … a kind of optical delusion of his consciousness.

That illusion is what breaks when you walk the Omega path. You stop seeing yourself as a separate self, trying to survive, and start experiencing yourself as a conscious part of the whole.

As Dr. David Hawkins taught:

> Every act of kindness, every inner shift toward love, every rise in consciousness, even in private life lifts the entire field of collective consciousness.

This path isn't just personal. When you heal, we all rise. It's like the tide that raises all boats. You will start contributing — helping to raise the tide. All boats will benefit. You'll join others who also work on themselves, producing the same byproducts for elevating humanity.

3. The Highs and Lows

Let's not pretend this path is all light, rainbows, and unicorns. It is not. There will be lows. I have felt many of them, and at times still do feel "lows." Now, for me, these lows are viewed through the lens of the Omega — not a person trying to prevent drowning in a soup of masculine perspective and imitation.

The Omega path will offer you some of the deepest highs of your life. Peace. Clarity. Even now, as described by Carl Jung. There will be moments when you feel so aligned, it's like the universe is breathing through you.

You'll experience powerful love — not the kind that hooks you or makes you feel attached to something, but the kind that holds you together. You'll feel a connection to life that doesn't depend on success, performance, or praise. You'll walk through a room and feel untouched by the noise and untouched by anyone's judgments or views about you. Not because you're above it but because you're rooted beneath it.

But there are lows, too. And they are real.

There will be moments of loneliness. Not the kind that comes from being unloved but from being unseen. From realizing that most of the world is no longer wired like you. You'll find it undesirable to be around certain people. It may feel daunting or like a "low". It's not that you'll think you're better, but because you may not resonate with them any longer. This type of low has an inkling of loneliness. It will fade. With practice, it will become a drive to continue and seek out like-minded, like-hearted people.

You may be misunderstood. You may be underestimated. You may be mocked, questioned, or written off. You'll feel the ache of being rare. You'll wonder who you are as your self-identity moves farther and farther away to nothing. And sometimes, you'll wonder if it's worth it.

But here's the key: the Omega doesn't avoid the lows. He holds them. He meets any pain without flinching. He meets confusion without collapsing. He meets disappointment without bargaining. He doesn't try to fix it, flee it, or dramatize it. He breathes into it. Because he knows that emotional steadiness isn't found by escaping pain; it's built by practicing

This is the difference between an Alpha or Sigma reaction and an Omega response. The Alpha reacts to pain with force. The Sigma with isolation. The Omega meets it with presence and gratitude.

You don't fight your way through suffering; you sit and analyze your way through it calmly, introspectively, with your practice, applying the Basics and the Playbook, changing old beliefs to new ones. That doesn't make you passive; it makes you unshakable.

When the highs come, you welcome them. When the lows come, you witness them. And in both, you remain yourself. The Omega path is not about perfection. It's about integrity under pressure. It's about being the same man in solitude as you are in success.

It's about learning to hold the full spectrum of life without letting it hijack your spirit.

4. Explain the Feeling

This is a beautiful terrain for metaphor. Becoming an Omega doesn't feel like winning. It feels like something else entirely.

- It feels like watching the storm but not being inside it.
- It feels like you've stopped needing to win the game, and that's when you start winning.
- It feels like being underwater; everything's quieter, heavier, and more real.
- Peacefulness begins to feel powerful.

It feels like stillness. It feels like peace — but not the kind that's fragile or fleeting. At first, peace can feel unsettling. Have you ever felt calm and thought, "this feels too good to be true"?

But Omega peace feels different. It doesn't buzz with anxiety. It doesn't wait to be interrupted. It feels grounded. Stable. Like you've come home not to a place but to yourself.

Don't get me wrong, the challenges still pop up — life never stops being life — but they show up less often. And when they do, they no longer knock you over, because the more authentic you become, the less there is to defend. There's no mask to protect. There's no script to remember to follow or forget. There's no ego to correct.

As I've moved from the scale of being an animal, from instinct to integrity, life hasn't become easier. It has, however, become clearer. With clarity comes safety — not from danger but from delusion.

To walk with these principles doesn't mean you float above problems. It means you face them with a new posture. One that's real. Sustainable. And filled with the highest degree of optimism under any circumstance.

That's what it feels like.

Living the ripple

This isn't just about becoming a better man. It's about becoming a man whose presence changes things. Not by force. Not by performance. But by example. You don't need to convince anyone that you are now YOU.

Your son notices. Your partner softens. Your friends pause before joking about something they used to think was funny. You haven't preached a word, but your presence said everything.

This is the ripple effect.

The ripple begins with you. It's not about performance but personal commitment — not to perfection, but to presence. To live intentionally.

To show up aligned even when it's hard. To let your choices speak louder than your story.

Yes, there will be resistance, both from the world and from inside you. You'll be tempted to go back. You'll question if it matters. That's when the ripple is working. You're no longer living for applause. You're living in alignment. And now, it's your turn. Not to teach. Not to convince. But to live. Quietly. Powerfully. Unapologetically.

This is the ripple. You heal, the world heals. You walk differently, and everyone feels it.

Chapter 12 wrap

This is the return.

Not simply a return to who you were, but a return to who you always were before the masks. Before the noise. Before the world told you what kind of man you had to be.

You don't need to shout it. You don't need to prove it. You only need to live it. The Omega Man doesn't come back to impress anyone. He comes back to embody something rare: stillness with a backbone. Kindness with conviction. A masculinity that doesn't need defending. This is what it means to return with the elixir. Not to save the world. But to become the kind of man who quietly makes it better just by walking through it.

You — the real you — returns home, now barefoot, after putting down the sword and the armor from battle, with stillness and with a backbone and air of internal invincibility.

Prelude to the conclusion: a moment to reflect

Before you close this book, I want you to pause. Take a breath. Think back to who you were when you first opened these pages. What were you carrying? What were you chasing? What were you avoiding? Who did you think you were?

Now ask yourself: How do I feel now? How do I feel in my chest? In my breath? In the space behind my eyes? Do I feel different?

Who do I think I am now?

Write it all down.

Capture the difference between then and now because that difference is the beginning of everything. You're not just reading a book anymore. You're rewriting the story of what it means to be a man, the story of what it means to be you.

And now, we begin the final chapter — the one only you can write.

Comments From Brad Kearns

If you've read this far, you have some ambition and enthusiasm and resolve to change your life. It hasn't been a light read by any means! But reading is just the first baby step to making things happen. That's why I appreciate the mention of "four ways resistance shows up": Fatigue, rationalization, avoidance, and doubt. The Four Horsemen of Failure! Oh man, can we all relate to these evil forces messing with our goals and dreams.

This is true today more than ever, because the digital world offers potential for nonstop distraction and instant gratification. Dave once gave me a fantastic and unforgettable tip on how to deal with stressful thoughts or situations: "Ask yourself, 'what should I be doing about this right now?' - nothing else matters", and that, "you better decide what to do, or life will decide for you."

If you don't take decisive action and use the skills you've learned in this book, you will most surely be taken down by fatigue, rationalization, avoidance and doubt. And you may not even realize it! You'll "convince yourself that your current situation isn't that bad;" you'll "stay busy with other things" and so forth.

I can totally relate to this as I've worked hard to cultivate a positive attitude and carefree spirit in life, which has sometimes actually been to my detriment. Why, you ask? As Dave explained to me, "fake acceptance, or fake gratitude, is a negative experience. Accepting a negative experience (not whitewashing) is a positive." I know there are worse problems out there then being "chill" in the face of life's challenges, but it's really not the correct play. For example, my fake acceptance of prolonged unfairness in a business partnership has landed me in a United States Federal Court lawsuit for breach of contract and theft of intellectual property. No fun, and something that could have been addressed with some skillful direct communication before things really got out of hand.

Take a moment to assess your current level of fatigue in daily life - maybe you can take some corrective action in the realms of diet, exercise and sleep? How about your penchant for rationalization - creating "smart-sounding reasons" - oh man, I know I'm busted there! How about avoidance? Look no further than your mobile device for evidence. Or in the workplace, doing busy work instead of going deep. And finally, if you're a bright and cheery type like me, let's consider whether we are convincing ourselves that our "current situation isn't that bad."

In the example of my messy lawsuit, I realize that I rationalized many red flags, avoided hard conversations, and convinced myself that things weren't that bad - and all that can be pretty fatiguing. Hey, I used all Four Horsemen in the same sentence!! Let's see if we can avoid that in real life.

Conclusion:

The Return of the Man Who Became Himself

Maybe you've noticed that this book blends evolutionary psychology, modern masculinity, self-awareness, relationships, survival instincts, philosophy, and cultural analysis. The goal was not just to critique the problem but to actively build a new framework. Building this new framework, i.e., a change in itself, is rare.

This book is designed to give you a clearer, more radical perspective than you've heard before. The Omega path is something that few understand, and few can teach. It is a collection of ancient texts, new teachings from modern thought leaders, scientific research, and personal experience. It seeks to synthesize spirituality, psychology, masculinity, and emotional evolution into something profoundly human and deeply earned.

What makes it powerful is that it's not coming from theory; it comes from blood, pain, love, loss, mistakes, and victories. That's a kind of intelligence and integration few, including AI, can understand. Statistics, studies, and large-scale data on human behavior can be processed by AI in vast quantities, but it can't live the kinds of moments that cracked me, and many others throughout history, wide open. It can't feel those lessons the way they were felt, and it can't teach them as they were lived, experienced, and survived. That's why this book shares and teaches ideals in a way that no data set, study, or algorithm ever could.

All this information exists out in the world, only in fragments that have never been pulled together in one place. The pain, the sadness, the loss, the discovery, the call to journey, the challenge, and the return, as Campbell calls it, are what wove into a single story.

The goal is to name the unspoken parts of modern masculinity — the hidden fears, the quiet shame, the unsaid truths — and to describe things many men feel but don't have words for. A further goal is to show the need to move beyond the Alpha/Sigma memes and offer a playbook for fundamental transformation — not just flipping the script, but writing an entirely new story.

Traditionally, if someone tried to create a new framework for male evolution based on what's been published, they would likely fall back on surface-level trends: emotional intelligence, stoicism, leadership psychology, and evolutionary biology. All good. However, these surface-level trends lack the most important thing: depth earned through experience, which you, too, have now been called to experience: To embark. To feel and experience the changes. To be challenged. And to return.

You should bring your own death into this, as Eckhart Tolle would request — not in a morbid way, but as a reminder that life's end is the greatest teacher. It teaches how to get yourself back spiritually, without dogma, and with self-esteem expressed now as authentic behavior. For you, too, this book speaks the quiet part out loud — that many men are dying emotionally because they're still living out a script from 68,000 BCE.

This is for you to turn the hero's journey inward, as I have experienced. What you may undertake is rare. Most dream about doing this. Some talk about doing this. Only a few actually do it.

The difference between dreaming, thinking, talking about, and doing it is becoming it. And that difference is everything. It is the line between living a story and living your life.

Through inner contemplation, I hope you've realized how rare it is for a man to walk this path, and how urgent, even sacred, it is that "more" begin.

Closing letter to the reader

If you're reading this, you made it. You stayed with me through the uncomfortable truths, the dismantling of old identities, and the peeling back of what it means to be a man in this world.

I want to thank you for your courage, for your curiosity, and for your willingness to look at the places most people spend a lifetime avoiding — the shadows, the doubts, the silence.

I started this book from a place of pain. I was still wiping the dust off my own collapse; financially, emotionally, spiritually. The roles I had played for decades had failed me. But in their failure, I saw the truth — I had never really chosen them. They were assigned. Programmed. Expected. Inherited.

Somewhere along the way, I stopped surviving and started awakening. Not overnight. Not in some glorious, movie-scene breakthrough. But day by day. Choice by choice. Breath by breath. I fell. I failed. I lost. And then I listened to the still, quiet voice inside me I had spent years ignoring.

I began to listen to the part of me that had no title, no label, no performance to maintain. The part that didn't need to win. The part that didn't need to be fixed. The Omega in me — quiet, steady, and finally free.

If this book gave you anything, I hope it was permission to stop performing, to stop proving, to stop pretending. To realize that the greatest strength you'll ever hold comes not from power, but from peace. Not from dominance, but from awareness. Not from chasing success but rather from choosing truth.

You don't need to be the Alpha. You just need to be real.

Here's what I know now — when you live from that place, when you stop climbing ladders that lead nowhere, you become something far more dangerous to the old systems. You become free. You become grounded. You become unshakable — not because you dominate, but because you no longer need to.

Maybe, like me, you'll look back at the burrow you crawled out of with gratitude. Not because it was fair, but because it shaped the man who finally chose to emerge.

This is your life. You get to define it now — not by old scripts, but by you.

As Nietzsche said: *"No price is too high to pay for the privilege of owning yourself."*

www.ingramcontent.com/pod-product-compliance
Lightning Source LLC
Chambersburg PA
CBHW070547160426
43199CB00014B/2410